Ours is a broken world, and suffering comes to us all. The cross stands as a painful reminder that not even the innocent escape it. Yet, the cross is also where mercy and truth met together, and righteousness and peace kissed each other; where light shone through darkness, and pain gave way to a glory that far outweighed it all. In his timely book, "*Beauty from the Ashes: Breaking Through the Pain Where Grace Will Sustain,*" my great friend, Dr. Mark Taylor, reminds us that the traumas we experience in this life offer new opportunities to meet Jesus in His sufferings, and find a grace sufficient, and strength perfected through weakness. In his words, "Your suffering is not wasted. Your story is not over ... Beauty is rising from ashes." Get this book! Read it! Keep it! Share it! What seems like an ending is only the beginning.

— Dr. Mark L. Williams, Third Assistant General Overseer
Church of God, Executive Committee

Like a seasoned captain steering through stormy seas, Mark Taylor guides readers of *Beauty from the Ashes* through the universal experience of pain and trauma, leading them on a healing journey toward renewal and empowering them to become healers themselves.

— Dr. Sean S. O'Neal, International Evangelism Director
Church of God, Ministry of Evangelism

Dr. Taylor has written a gem that brings a Biblical fresh approach on the topic of trauma. As someone who has spent the last 15 years of his life as a professional counselor for ministerial families, I will be recommending *Beauty from the Ashes* to future clients. It is truly a great addition to anyone's library.

— Dr. Tim Maness, Spiritual Care Director/Counselor,
Church of God, Center for Ministrial Care

Through transparency and openness regarding personal painful events in his life, Dr. Mark Taylor takes you on a journey towards healing in his book, *Beauty from the Ashes.* This book will reaffirm and show you that when you apply God's Word in awareness of your own circumstance, along with implementation of concrete principles, you too can realize God's mercy and grace and see the beauty in your ashes.

— Pastor Deena Querry, Senior Pastor
Living Waters Christian Fellowship, Fountain Valley, CA

Beauty from the Ashes is more than a book—it is a testimony to the transforming power of God's grace in the midst of deep personal loss and brokenness. Mark Taylor doesn't just tell his story; he invites us into the holy ground of grief, redemption, and hope. With pastoral depth and Spirit-formed wisdom, he walks readers through the fire and shows how even the most painful chapters can become sacred ground for growth.

As a Certified Trainer with LeaderLabs, Mark has equipped others with tools for leadership and resilience. But in this book, he opens his own life as the lesson—and it's one of the most powerful trainings he's ever offered. I believe *Beauty from the Ashes* will bring healing to the hurting, clarity to the confused, and courage to those wondering if God can still write beauty into their story.

I wholeheartedly recommend this book to leaders, pastors, and anyone walking through the ashes—because what God has done for Mark, He can do for you.

— Dr. Fred Garmon, Founder, LeaderLabs
Organizational Leadership, PhD

BEAUTY FROM THE ASHES

Breaking Through the Pain Where Grace Will Sustain

Mark A. Taylor, DMin, LPCC

BOW
Breathe Out Worship
PRINT & MUSIC PUBLISHING

Published by Breathe Out Worship Print & Music Puslishing

1020 W. Grove Avenue, Visalia, CA 93291, 559 510 0747

ISBN: 979-8-9931772-0-5

Cover Design & Interior Layout: M. Taylor and M. Christian

Printed in the United States of America

Contents

Dedications

To ***Christy Taylor***, my wife, who is a living testament to God's grace and mercy, reminding me that His redemption never leaves a life in ruin.

To ***Dr. Oliver McMahan*** (1954-2024), who instilled in me the confidence to embrace my calling and vocation, walking in an anointing, empathy, and compassion.

Acknowledgements

To my loving wife, ***Christy Taylor***—thank you for the countless nights you patiently listened as I shared the concept and read these pages aloud again and again. Your unwavering support, grace, and presence gave this book its heartbeat.

To Mama & Daddy, ***Pastor C.J. (Joe) & Helen Taylo***r thank you for leading me to believe in Jesus and for never giving up on me.

To my brother, ***Pastor Johnny Taylor***—thank you for being the "question asker"who challenges my thinking and pushes me to see truth and fresh perspectives. Your wisdom and courage sharpen me, and I am grateful for your voice in my life.

To my sister, ***Kimberly Baker***, LCSW—thank you for being my greatest cheerleader, especially in the moments when I didn't believe in myself. Your encouragement helped carry me through.

To ***Dr. Darla Cuadra***—thank you for your friendship and for the many days you graciously let me bounce ideas off of you. Your insight and support have been an invaluable part of this journey.

To ***Pastor Michael Christian*** for your kindness and tremendous support in formating this book for publication.

To the Brotherhood:
Jeff Wilson, Geoff Osborne, Jose Cruz, & Tim Kirkendall
You guys have always been there for me—even when I didn't deserve it. I am forever grateful.

Foreword

We have all experienced trouble at one time or another. If you haven't…just wait. It is coming. Escaping it is inevitable because we live in a broken world. Trouble comes in many different shapes and sizes. It varies in intensity. It varies in duration. We call it different things. But it affects us just the same. While we would like to keep it at bay, there is no avoiding seeing it wreak havoc in our lives. It usually comes without warning, storming in and stealing the focus of life.

Although we shouldn't live our lives expecting trouble we shouldn't be surprised when it comes. Jesus said in Matthew 5:45, "…He causes his sun to rise on the evil and the good, and sends rain on the righteous and the unrighteous." When it rains, everyone gets wet. As much as we would like to escape its grasp it always seems to rush in, do its damage, and, just as quickly, it is over.

The real issue is not the avoidance of trouble; it is how we walk through it. Many, especially those in ministry, do not handle it well. Some appear to do just fine – and maybe they do. But many, if the trauma is intense enough, suffer long-lasting damage. Their lives seem to be overshadowed by the chaos that turned their lives upside down. It doesn't matter how much they try to get past it…the memory of the circumstances seems to anchor them to that point in their lives. Many feel that they must live with the pain and hurt because it just will not go away.

No one really understands the gravity of what life can bring. Everyone makes plans and is shocked and surprised when those plans are derailed and, sometimes, crushed right in front of you. While some would say it is just how life works, it never lessens the pain of seeing your hopes and dreams crumble to the ground. Standing amidst the ashes of broken dreams and crushed plans, we wonder if recovery and healing is possible.

Dr. Taylor has seen his share of traumatic circumstances. I know because we walked through many of them together. As one of my closest friends in this world we laughed and cried as we walked through life (and still do) together. We shared in the joys of being in each other's weddings, watching our kids grow up, and sharing in ministry experiences. He walked with me through the sorrow of my first daughter's pre-mature birth and subsequent death. The hurt and pain seemed too much to bear. He has walked through similar situations and experienced his own pain and sorrow. These life experiences coupled with his deep love for God and his passion for ministry has allowed him to not only survive but to thrive. It has given him a heart for those who have been affected by traumatic circumstances in life. The result is *Beauty from the Ashes*.

In this book, Dr. Taylor walks us through the steps of not just dealing with trauma; we learn how to overcome it. He draws from extensive research and experiences to paint a beautiful picture of hope and healing. Understanding that recognizing trauma is the beginning of the journey, Dr. Taylor explains that life and ministry aren't over because of our brokenness. He draws from real-world examples to take us on a journey that many think isn't possible after such pain. It is a must read for anyone that has experienced or is experiencing trouble or trauma and you just can't seem to break free of its grip. The Biblical and real-life examples step us through what trauma is, how to recognize it, and how to stop it from controlling our lives. It is practical, needed, and necessary. As an additional resource there are reflection questions at the end of every chapter to help us all recognize what we are currently walking through, identify it, and deal with it.

If you or anyone you know is dealing with trouble or trauma of any kind, I encourage you to continue reading. You won't be disappointed, and you may just find yourself starting the healing journey that you have been looking for. God bless you.

— Jeff Wilson Lead Pastor,
Elevate Life Church, Saint Peters, MO.

Author of *40 Days at the Well* and *Evading Trouble*

Preface

Trauma, an experience that produces psychological injury or pain, is a relative term when it comes to our emotional and mental health. Somewhere, somehow, somebody has hurt us. Some people hold onto emotional trauma far too long, while others do not hold on to it long enough. The one undeniable truth for those who have experienced it is that God is right there in the middle of our pain, just as surely as He stood in the flames with three Hebrew adolescents. He does not abandon us in our suffering. Instead, He walks with us, refining us through the fire, not consuming us in it.

Furthermore, everyone will experience a gut-wrenching, sleepless night, crying out, "When will this end?" kind of pain. Why aren't we better prepared for it? Why do we so often take on the blame, shame, and name of "loser" after we encounter such hurt? It would be easy to assume that our pain is a result of not praying well enough, or worse, to convince ourselves that it's our fault for allowing certain people into our lives. Some of us even protect those who have wounded us, thinking that shielding them from judgment somehow shields us from more pain. But the truth remains: God does not see us as failures. Rather, He sees us as works in progress, vessels He is shaping, redeeming, and molding through the power of the Holy Spirit.

There it is in a nutshell—we *will* experience pain, but we will only make it through with God's provision. He does not want us to fall away from our relationship with Him or from others. Instead, He wants to build us up again and see our relationships flourish. He desires to cultivate a new crop of testimonies in us—stories of healing and redemption that we can share with others who have felt the cutting edge of trauma's sharp knife. This is where the idea for this book came into being.

Isaiah's words in Isaiah 61:3 became a source of encouragement during the most difficult times of my life. Over and over, I found myself returning to that passage, clinging to its promise that beauty would rise from the ashes of my broken heart and life. Eventually, I began to see how God was bringing people into my life who were hurting just like me. I realized He wanted me to commit these words to print—not for my sake, but for the sake of those who have ever been emotionally damaged by life's seemingly insurmountable tests.

The years leading up to the decision to write *Beauty from the Ashes* were significant. For so long, I had focused on Isaiah 61:3, missing the greater picture. But as I reread it in its full context, my heart pounded with excitement, my lips curved into a smile, and my eyes filled with tears. Suddenly, I was transported back in time.

I was thirteen years old, sitting in a California/Nevada Regional Camp Meeting service in Bakersfield, California. Dr. Lamar Vest was the speaker that night, and when he gave the altar call, he called me over. He looked at me and confirmed what I had already felt stirring in my heart—that God was calling me to ministry. It wasn't because the call to preach ran in my family, but because God had personally placed His hand on my life. From that night on, Luke 4:18-19 became an anchor Scripture for me. I would often read and hear those words, and they would bring me to my knees in submission to the calling God had placed on my life. But years later, my understanding would shift—laser-focused on one phrase: "to set at liberty them that are bruised."

It hit me. I was the bruised one. And yet, God was calling me to help others find their liberty. That realization changed everything. I had always wanted to preach to the poor, to bring healing to the brokenhearted, and to help restore those who had lost their way. But now I understood something deeper—to minister to the broken, I had to first understand what it meant to be broken myself.

Isaiah 61:1-2 marked Phase One of my life—a time when I knew I was called but had not yet walked through the valleys that would shape me. I had no idea that Phase Two would be ushered in through some of the most painful seasons of my life. Sitting in my study years later, reflecting on the words of Isaiah 61:3, I realized something profound: God had been preparing me all along.

Hopefully, as you read these words, the Lord is bringing you into your own Phase Two, where you are beginning to see that there is more to life than Trauma's pain. Either way, do not lose heart! I can say with confidence that if you open your eyes to His healing and purpose, you will see beauty rise from your ashes.

The Bible is replete with men and women who have faced triumphs and victories, highs and lows, mountains and valleys. Since the Fall of Man, trauma has been a thematic thread linking all our favorite Bible heroes and antiheroes alike. King Saul fell into a deep depressive state as he was tormented by an oppressive spirit. King David responded to his trauma by writing psalms of lament and worship, turning his pain into poetry that still resonates with believers today. Elijah, after a great victory, fled in fear and sat under a tree, begging God to take his life. Job, a man who lost everything, struggled to understand his suffering yet was ultimately restored beyond measure. Trauma is a foe that must be fought as a team—with the Triune God as our support, and with the honest, healthy choices we make toward recovery.

Trauma affects everything—our ability to minister effectively, cope with life's hardships, utilize recovery skills, and embrace true forgiveness and peace. But healing is possible. That healing comes through:

- Forgiveness to move forward
- Peace to settle in
- Living life to the fullest
- Giving hope to others

This was the task given to me through my own traumatic journey—to lean on Jesus, grow in Jesus, and give out Jesus to the bruised souls within reach of my influence.

Beauty from the Ashes is about far more than my story. It's about you, the reader. It's about the Savior, the One who alone can take what has been broken and restore it to wholeness. It's about the God who does not allow our suffering to be wasted, but instead, transforms it into something beautiful. If you are walking through the fire today, hold on. The flames will not consume you. Your beauty from the ashes is coming.

— Dr. Mark A. Taylor, D.Min, LPCC #19467

BEAUTY FROM THE ASHES

Breaking Through the Pain Where Grace Will Sustain

1

TRAUMATIZED

Everyone has a story where trauma enters their life. Mine was no different.

Everyone has a story where trauma enters their life. Mine was no different. I remember vividly the moment that changed everything. "I don't have the feelings it takes to be married to you anymore." Those were the words I read as I fell into the most devastating emotional trauma I had ever known. Divorce was not in the plans for either my former wife or myself, yet there we were—both hurt from each other, both hurting each other. I kept asking myself, "How could this be happening to me?" It's a question that lingers in the minds of everyone who experiences deep pain, replaying over and over as they try to make sense of their own version of trauma.

Blame and shame are key players in this game where nobody seems to win. It makes sense, really. The enemy of our souls would like nothing more than to "steal, kill, and destroy" all that God has purposed for our lives. He seeks to spiritually abort any redeemable value, to leave us broken, abandoned, and questioning whether our calling can survive the wreckage. And that's exactly how I felt—like my life had been reduced to a heap of smoldering ashes.

Abandonment and loneliness. Darkness and despair. The most traumatic experience of my life. Hurt was just another ordinary word until I found myself driving to and from work every day, sobbing uncontrollably, wailing to God about the predicament I was in. What would others think? More importantly, what did God think of me? I was a failure who had brought shame to my family, my calling, and my Savior. The redeemable qualities of my life seemed to diminish into an unredeemable river of pain. Have you ever felt that way? If you're reading this book, chances are, you have.

Back then, I was in Phase One of a deeper calling and didn't even realize it. When God first called me into ministry in 1983, He often used Luke 4:18-19 to get my attention. Jesus was reading Isaiah 61:1-2 from the scroll, declaring His mission to "heal the brokenhearted, preach deliverance to the captives, and set at liberty them that are bruised." I was humbled every time I heard those words, and I knew the Spirit of the Lord was upon me, too. I longed to walk in that anointing—to preach to the poor, to bring healing to the brokenhearted, to help open blind eyes. I wanted to do all these things and more.

But then, my world fell apart. Now it was all over. At least, that's what I thought. But little did I know that in the next ten years of my life, I would go from seeing my life as a figurative wreck to a purposeful life of redemption. The Prince of Peace would restore a peace beyond understanding, placing a guard over my heart and mind (Philippians 4:7). Eventually, I would experience a breakthrough from the pain where His grace would sustain me, bringing back a life that, as the prophet Joel described, the cankerworm had seemingly eaten.

Then it all became clear as I pondered Isaiah 61:1-2. The Lord had been directing my path for His name's sake all along. He was restoring me from a broken person into someone who could walk with the broken. By the Holy Spirit's anointing, I was to "heal the brokenhearted and set at liberty them that are bruised." But living out such a ministry requires more than good intentions—it demands intimate knowledge of what it means to be broken and bruised. It requires endurance, obedience, and a willingness to be poured out for the sake of others.

No one wants a "know-it-all" to speak into their lives when they're hurting. They want to hear from someone who knows what brokenness feels like. Someone who has been crushed but still stands. Someone who can minister from a place of personal experience and the compassion of Christ, who said, "Neither do I condemn you" (John 8:11).

If Phase One was about breaking me down to build me up, then Phase Two was about filling me up to pour me out. God's plan for my life has never been easy. Quite honestly, I have made messes over and over again. But through those messes, I have learned how to be a ship on the sea—steady in course and clear in direction.

During this painful season, I was grateful for the wisdom of Bishop Charles Fischer, who served as Administrative Bishop in the Church of God California/Nevada region. He became a mentor I desperately needed, reminding me that my calling did not end because of a blip on the screen of my life. Instead, this trial was an opportunity for growth.

We all have individuals in our lives who make us better. The most important person who has influenced my faith, calling, and vocation is also the most supportive person in my life—Christy Taylor, my wife. When my first marriage ended, I thought I would never be loved again, let alone preach again. I assumed I would always be branded and unwanted.

But my "beauty from the ashes" moment came when this beautiful woman, inside and out, stepped into my life. She loved me unconditionally. She accepted my children as her own. She chose to walk this journey of ministry, not as a passive observer, but as a co-laborer called by God in her own right.

For the past thirteen years, my life has been filled with joy, peace, and every other fruit of the Spirit. I am becoming a better man—a Christ-follower, a husband, a father, a pastor, a therapist, and overall, a better person. It is humbling to know that the Lord loves me without fail and is faithful to His promises. Living out this calling and vocation is truly a dream come true. It is clearly the desire of my heart.

The reality is, everyone will experience trauma. The severity of that trauma may vary from person to person, but it is still trauma to them. Many people work tirelessly to control everything around them, hoping to avoid ever being hurt again. But the problem with this type of thinking is that pain will come again. The Psalmist reminds us of the "many afflictions of the righteous" (Psalm 34:19, ESV), and James speaks of the "various kinds of trials" (James 1:2, ESV). Yet, we often miss the point: we can overcome and be delivered from a broken heart because the Lord is near to us.

Trauma is viewed differently by each individual, shaped by their personal history, experiences, and perceptions. Western culture often seeks to control trauma rather than allow the Holy Spirit to lead us through it. But sometimes, God requires us to climb the mountain instead of going around it. There are lessons to learn in the climb. There are skills to be honed in the valley. There are moments of growth we will never experience unless we hold His hand and walk the journey of trauma with Him instead of resisting His leading.

So, let me ask you: What trauma are you trying to hide from? What baggage are you carrying that is weighing you down? Are you ready to surrender it to the One who heals?

As we move forward, it is important to define what trauma actually is. It is a deeply distressing or disturbing experience that often follows a stressful event, sometimes leading to long-term emotional, psychological, or even physical effects. Trauma can be externally induced (caused by others) or internally induced (our own failures and choices).

Consider King David. He faced both types of traumas—first as a young man, relentlessly pursued by King Saul, and later as a king himself, after causing his own suffering through sin with Bathsheba and the murder of Uriah. Even after these events, David endured betrayal by his own son, Absalom. Yet, his response to trauma was key—he sought God's wisdom during external struggles and repented earnestly when he was the cause of his own pain (Psalm 51).

Trauma is inevitable. The real question is, how will we handle it? Healthy individuals learn to forgive themselves and others. But for those who are just beginning their journey of recovery and restoration, this process takes time. It takes patience. And it takes an unshakable trust in the God who turns ashes into beauty.

Ministers and Trauma: A Silent Battle

As I have studied, counseled, and walked with other ministers, I have come to understand that the journey of trauma is especially complex for those in ministry. In my dissertation, *A Summary of Ministers with Trauma and Their Journey to Trauma Recovery and Greater Success in Their Ministry Context,* I examined the impact of trauma on pastors, ministry leaders, and church workers. What I found was both heartbreaking and revealing: many ministers suffer in silence, carrying deep wounds while continuing to lead others.

Ministry can be one of the most rewarding yet isolating callings. Pastors often experience betrayal, burnout, and loss, but few are given the space to grieve, process, or heal. We preach healing to others while struggling to believe it for ourselves. There is an unspoken expectation that pastors should be immune to trauma, that faith should be enough to sustain us through every trial. Yet, countless ministers have experienced emotional breakdowns, moral failures, or have simply walked away from their calling—not because they didn't love God, but because they were too broken to continue.

As I sat in my own grief, wrestling with my sense of failure and shame, I came to realize that my journey was not just about me—it was about every minister who had ever wondered, "Can God still use me after this?"

The Reality of Brokenness

For many of us, trauma feels unfair. We assume that faithfulness to God will somehow shield us from suffering. But Job's story in the Bible reminds us that even the righteous will endure deep pain.

Job was a man of integrity and devotion to God. He was wealthy, respected, and had a family he deeply loved. Yet, in a sudden and tragic turn of events, Job lost everything—his children, his livestock, his servants, and his health (Job 1-2).

What's even more staggering is that Job's suffering was not due to his sin, but because God allowed it to test his faith. The enemy sought to destroy Job's trust in God, believing that if enough pain was inflicted, Job would curse Him.

As Job sat in his brokenness, covered in sores and mourning his losses, his friends tried to explain why this was happening. They told him he must have done something to deserve it, that his suffering was punishment from God.

How many of us have felt like Job? How many of us have sat in the ashes of our suffering, wondering why God would allow us to endure such deep pain? How many of us have had people—well-meaning or otherwise—try to explain our suffering, offering shallow answers that only deepen our wounds?

Yet, the beauty of Job's story is that his suffering was not the end. In Job 42, we see a powerful moment of restoration. God not only speaks to Job, reminding him of His sovereignty, but He blesses Job beyond what he had before. His latter days were greater than his former days.

That is the nature of God's redemptive work—He does not simply return what was lost; He multiplies His blessings.

I have come to understand that God does not just allow suffering—He redeems it. He takes our most painful experiences and transforms them into testimonies that glorify Him. A song I have come to know, and love is a song by the Gospel group, Selah, called, *Unredeemed*. In essence, the song shares that in life, some places feel broken or unfinished. Yet God's grace is already moving there. What seems lost is never beyond His reach. If we wait and watch, His miracle will unfold. Nothing in His hands remains unredeemed.

Takeway: Trauma Does Not Define Us-God's Purpose is Greater.

One of the biggest lies Trauma tells us is that our pain is the final chapter of our story. It whispers that we will never be whole again, that our suffering has disqualified us from purpose, that we are forever marked by what has happened to us. But God tells a different story.

Like Job, Joseph, and David, we are not defined by our suffering—we are defined by God's purpose for our lives. Pain is never the end of the story when God is the Author.

I once believed my trauma had destroyed me. I thought I had lost everything—my family, my reputation, my ministry. But I was wrong. God was not finished with me. He was rebuilding, restoring, and repurposing my pain into something far greater than I could have imagined.

And the same is true for you. Your suffering is not wasted. Your story is not over. Your brokenness does not define you—God's purpose does. So whatever trauma you have walked through, whatever pain you are still carrying, know this: God is not done with you yet.

He is still working.
He is still writing.
And beauty is rising from the ashes.
Will you trust Him with your story?

Reflection Questions for Chapter 1

Personal Reflection on Trauma

1. Reflect on a moment in your life when trauma entered your story. How did it impact your emotions, thoughts, and relationships?

2. Dr. Taylor shares how trauma made him feel like his life was "a heap of smoldering ashes." Have you ever felt like your purpose was destroyed by pain? If so, how?

Spiritual and Biblical Reflection

3. Isaiah 61:1-3 speaks about God's promise to bring "beauty from ashes." How does this promise bring hope to your own story?

4. Romans 8:28 declares that "God works all things together for good for those who love Him." How can you trust that God is working—even through your pain?

Healing and Moving Forward

5. Healing often requires surrendering our trauma to God. What is one step you can take today to begin that surrender process?

6. What does it mean for you to trust God with your story? How can you allow Him to take your pain and repurpose it for something greater?

2

SUPERSIZED

Problems seem to get bigger and bigger as we focus on them.

There is a natural human tendency to magnify what we focus on. The more attention we give to a problem, the larger it appears. What begins as a moment of fear, pain, or uncertainty can quickly turn into an overwhelming crisis simply because we fixate on it. Unchecked trauma, anxiety, and self-doubt thrive when given too much mental real estate.

In *The Caring Christian,* McMahan and Hughes (1996) emphasize that the way we process trauma is deeply influenced by the support systems around us. They highlight that when individuals experience personal crises—whether loss, betrayal, or burnout—the perception of suffering often becomes more overwhelming than the actual event itself. When left unchecked, our minds enlarge pain, making it seem as though healing is impossible.

This is especially true for ministers who often suffer in silence, believing they must carry their burdens alone. In my dissertation, *A Summary of Ministers with Trauma and Their Journey to Trauma Recovery,* I found that many pastors magnify their struggles to the point that they seem insurmountable. Ministry wounds, failures, and disappointments begin to overshadow the calling, purpose, and promises of God.

The danger of magnification is that it distorts reality. It convinces us that our pain is greater than God's power. It tells us that our trauma is too big to be redeemed. It deceives us into believing that our suffering is the final word. But God's truth stands in opposition to this deception.

The Danger of Magnification

As stated earlier, the mind has a way of enlarging problems, making them appear insurmountable. What begins as a manageable issue can quickly escalate into intense hardship when our focus remains fixed on the struggle rather than the solution. The greater our attention to the problem, the more distorted and consuming it becomes. Research has shown that unchecked stress, anxiety, and negative thought patterns can amplify emotional distress, leading to cognitive distortions that impact perception and decision-making (McMahan, 1999).

This is especially true for those in ministry. In my research (Taylor, 2023), it was found that many ministers suffer in silence, allowing their unresolved trauma to dictate their effectiveness in ministry. When their focus remains on past wounds, betrayals, or failures, these experiences grow larger in their minds, eclipsing any sense of hope, healing, or renewal.

Magnification leads to:

- ***Burnout*** – A growing sense of exhaustion and emotional depletion.
- ***Spiritual paralys***is – The inability to lead or minister effectively due to overwhelming guilt or shame.

- *Isolation* – Withdrawal from community and relationships due to the belief that no one understands.
- *Loss of faith* – A shifting perception of God's ability to redeem pain.

McMahan (1999) highlights that one of the greatest needs within the Church is a culture that acknowledges pain without magnifying it. Yet, pastors and church leaders often lack a structured support system when they themselves are in crisis. Without the necessary emotional and spiritual care, they are left to internally magnify their own struggles, reinforcing the false belief that they are beyond help or restoration.

The Mental Toll of Unchecked Pain

Unchecked pain, particularly trauma that remains unprocessed, leads to significant cognitive and emotional consequences. Negative emotions that are continually dwelt upon contribute to increased stress, anxiety, and depression (McMahan, 1999; Taylor, 2023).

When trauma is left unresolved, its impact deepens:

Rumination is one of the most deceptive traps of trauma. It is the tendency to overanalyze problems, replaying painful events over and over in our minds, making them appear even larger than they are. Instead of moving forward, we become stuck in a cycle of "what ifs" and "if onlys," magnifying our suffering until it feels insurmountable. This constant dwelling on the past fuels anxiety, depression, and self-doubt, keeping us from embracing our healing. Scripture warns against this pattern, encouraging believers to instead dwell on what is true, noble, and praiseworthy (Philippians 4:8, NIV). When we surrender our thoughts to God, we begin to break free from the endless loop of negativity that trauma so often creates.

Emotional exhaustion is another consequence of unprocessed pain. When we carry the weight of trauma without addressing it, our minds and bodies begin to wear down. The joy we once had fades, motivation dwindles, and even the simplest tasks feel overwhelming. This exhaustion is more than just physical fatigue—it seeps into our spiritual and emotional well-being, making it difficult to connect with God and others. Elijah experienced this after his encounter on Mount Carmel. Fear and despair drained him, leaving him so weary that he prayed for God to take his life (1 Kings 19:4). Yet, God met him with rest, nourishment, and reassurance. Emotional exhaustion is real, but it is not the end of the story. When we allow God to replenish us, He gives us the strength to keep going.

Fear-driven decision-making keeps us paralyzed, preventing us from stepping into healing or pursuing what God has for us. Trauma distorts our perception of reality, making our problems seem bigger than they actually are. This leads to avoidance—avoiding relationships, ministry, opportunities, and even God—out of fear that we will be hurt again. Like Peter walking on water, fear causes us to sink when we take our eyes off Jesus and focus on the storm (Matthew 14:30). Healing requires us to shift our focus from fear to faith, trusting that God is greater than our past pain and that He is guiding us toward wholeness.

Distorted perception of self is one of the most damaging effects of trauma. It convinces us that we are not enough, that we are unworthy of love, and that our failures define us. When wounds go unhealed, they shape how we see ourselves, making it difficult to accept God's grace and believe in His purpose for our lives. This is exactly what happened to Moses when he doubted his ability to lead (Exodus 4:10-12). He saw himself as inadequate, but God saw him as chosen. Trauma does not get to determine our identity—God does. When we allow Him to renew our minds, we begin to see ourselves through His eyes: redeemed, restored, and deeply loved.

Ministers experience an intense psychological burden, as they are expected to care for others while struggling silently with their own pain (Taylor, 2023). This internal struggle exacerbates the problem, making the storm feel larger than it is. This is what happened to Peter in Matthew 14:22-33.

Peter and the disciples were caught in a storm. As waves battered their boat, they saw Jesus walking toward them on the water. Initially afraid, Peter boldly asked Jesus, "Lord, if it is you, command me to come to you on the water" (Matthew 14:28, ESV). When Jesus told him to come, Peter did the impossible—he walked on water.

However, as soon as Peter shifted his focus from Jesus to the storm, he began to sink. The waves had always been there, but his perception of them changed. The moment he magnified the danger rather than the presence of Jesus, he lost faith and began to drown.

The principle is clear:
What we magnify will control us.

- If we focus on the waves, we will sink.
- If we focus on Jesus, we will stand.

McMahan (1999) underscores that the Church must be a place that helps people redirect their focus toward Christ rather than their struggles. However, ministers often struggle without a structured system of care, leading them to feel as though they are sinking with no lifeline in sight.

Super-Sizing Our Problems: The Enemy's Strategy

The enemy actively seeks to magnify wounds, failures, and fears. Satan's strategy is to steal, kill, and destroy (John 10:10), and one of his most effective tactics is to distort perception.

One of the most damaging lies that trauma tells ministers is that they are too broken to ever be restored. After experiencing deep wounds—whether from betrayal, burnout, or personal failure—it is easy to believe that healing is impossible. Ministry, by its very nature, requires vulnerability, and when that vulnerability is met with pain instead of support, the scars can feel permanent. However, Scripture tells a different story. Throughout the Bible, God used broken people—Moses, who doubted himself; David, who fell into moral failure; Peter, who denied Christ. None of them were beyond redemption, and neither are we. Psalm 147:3 (ESV) reminds us that God "heals the brokenhearted and binds up their wounds." No matter how deep the trauma, His grace is greater.

Another false narrative that keeps ministers trapped in trauma is the belief that no one will ever trust them again. Whether the wound comes from personal mistakes or from being falsely accused, the enemy capitalizes on broken relationships to isolate leaders. The fear of never being trusted again can cause ministers to withdraw, avoiding community rather than risking further pain. However, trust is not built overnight, and it is not restored by retreating in fear. Even Paul, who once persecuted the church, was eventually accepted by the apostles (Acts 9:26-27) because he continued to walk in obedience despite the skepticism of others. Healing requires patience, but when we remain faithful, God can restore even the most fractured relationships.

A particularly crippling distortion is the thought that past failure has disqualified us from ministry. Many ministers who have walked through moral failure, burnout, or crisis struggle to believe that they can ever be used by God again. Shame convinces them that they are no longer fit for their calling, leading them to step away from ministry entirely. Yet, failure does not disqualify us—unwillingness to heal does. Peter denied Christ three times, but Jesus restored him and called him to feed His sheep (John 21:15-17). God's mercy does not erase consequences, but it does provide a pathway to redemption. He does not abandon His calling on our lives because of our mistakes; rather, He uses those failures to shape us into more compassionate, grace-filled leaders.

Perhaps the most haunting thought is that we will never be the same after this loss. Trauma changes us, but it does not have to define us. The belief that we are permanently damaged often leads to bitterness and despair, robbing us of the hope that God can bring beauty from ashes. Joseph endured betrayal, false accusations, and years of imprisonment, yet he emerged with a heart that still trusted in God's sovereignty (Genesis 50:20). Healing does not mean returning to who we were before the trauma—it means becoming stronger, wiser, and more deeply rooted in God's grace. We may not be the same, but through Christ, we can be even more equipped for the work He has called us to do.

I found that ministers who successfully moved from trauma to recovery did so by shifting their focus from their wounds to God's ability to redeem. Those who remained stuck in pain and self-doubt did not necessarily experience greater trauma, but they focused on their wounds rather than on healing.

McMahan (1999) adds that when the Church becomes a place of healing and support rather than judgment and rejection, ministers are more likely to find restoration. This requires intentional care structures that offer counseling, mentoring, and spiritual guidance.

Takeaway: Redirecting Focus from Problems to God's Promises.

The greatest shift that can occur for any minister or believer struggling with overwhelming pain is the realization that our focus determines our outcome.

Like Peter, we have a choice:

Focus on the waves – our failures, disappointments, and fears. Or, focus on Jesus – the One who called, sustains, and redeems us.

The solution is not to deny the reality of suffering or pretend that it doesn't exist, but rather to view it through the lens of God's promises rather than our own limitations. Pain and hardship are an unavoidable part of life, and Scripture does not shy away from this truth. Instead, it offers reassurance that while trouble is inevitable, God's presence, grace, and strength are constant. He does not leave us to struggle alone, nor does He expect us to overcome adversity in our own strength.

When we face intense struggles, personal failures, or ministry burnout, we can either magnify the weight of our burdens or shift our focus toward the promises of God. His Word repeatedly reminds us that no matter how broken we feel, His faithfulness never wavers, and His power is made perfect in our weakness. By redirecting our perspective from our trials to the truth of God's sustaining grace, we find hope, healing, and the courage to move forward, knowing that restoration is not only possible but promised.

God's Presence in the Storm

> *"When you pass through the waters, I will be with you; and through the rivers, they shall not overwhelm you."*
>
> —Isaiah 43:2 (ESV)

Isaiah 43:2 is a direct promise from God to His people in exile, reminding them that difficult seasons are inevitable, but they will not be destroyed. The imagery of passing through waters and rivers points back to the Israelites crossing the Red Sea (Exodus 14) and the Jordan River (Joshua 3). In both cases, the people of God faced seemingly impossible obstacles—yet God made a way where there seemed to be no way.

For ministers dealing with trauma, this verse is a reminder that hardship does not equal abandonment. The waters will come, but they will not consume us. The rivers will rise, but they will not overpower us—because God Himself is walking with us. Our survival does not depend on our own strength but on the One who holds the waters back.

When struggles in ministry or life threaten to overwhelm us, it is easy to feel as though we are drowning—pulled under by fear, uncertainty, and exhaustion. The weight of responsibility, personal failures, and painful experiences can make the waters seem impossibly deep, leaving us gasping for air, searching for relief. In those moments, the temptation is to focus solely on the size of the waves rather than on the One who has power over them. Yet, throughout Scripture, God reminds us that no storm is too fierce, no river too wide, and no hardship too great for Him to overcome. He does not promise a life without trials, but He does promise that we will never face them alone. His presence is constant, His strength unshaken, and His victory already secured. Even when the waters seem to rise around us, threatening to consume us, we must shift our perspective from drowning in fear to trusting in His unfailing faithfulness. The circumstances may not change immediately, and the storm may not pass as quickly as we would hope, but we can stand firm in the truth that God has already declared victory over every struggle we will ever face. When we fix our eyes on Him rather than on the overwhelming flood before us, we find that His presence sustains us, His grace empowers us, and His love carries us safely through to the other side.

Strength in Weakness

> *"My grace is sufficient for you, for my power is made perfect in weakness."*
>
> —2 Corinthians 12:9

In 2 Corinthians 12:9 (ESV), Paul recounts his struggle with a "thorn in the flesh"—a persistent hardship that he begged God to remove. Instead of granting immediate relief, God reassured Paul that His grace was enough, and divine power is evident when human strength runs out.

Many ministers who experience trauma or burnout struggle with feelings of inadequacy, believing they must always be strong. However, Paul's revelation turns this expectation upside down—weakness is not a disqualification, but an invitation for God's power to work through us.

When ministry feels overwhelming, instead of asking, "Why am I so weak?", we can ask, "How can God's strength be revealed through my weakness?" His grace is sufficient—not just in seasons of clarity, but especially in seasons of uncertainty.

A Refuge in Crisis

> *"God is our refuge and strength, a very present help in trouble."*
>
> —Psalm 46:1 (ESV)

Psalm 46:1 paints a picture of God as a shelter in life's storms. The word "refuge" suggests a fortified place of safety, while "strength" implies an active source of power. The phrase "very present help" emphasizes that God is not distant in trouble—He is right there in the midst of it.

For ministers walking through trauma, this verse speaks directly to the fear of facing struggles alone. Too often, leaders isolate themselves in times of pain, believing they must handle their burdens alone. But Psalm 46:1 reminds us that God is not only present but actively providing the strength we need.

Instead of retreating in fear or exhaustion, we must take refuge in God, recognizing that He is both a place of safety and a source of strength. His presence is not a last resort but a constant reality in our suffering.

When our problems feel super-sized, the only way to shrink them is by magnifying the promises of God instead of our circumstances. The storm will come, the waves will rise, and the waters may seem deep—but if we keep our eyes on God's presence, His grace, and His strength, we will not be overcome.

McMahan (1999) challenges the Church to become the vessel through which healing takes place. The role of a caring church is not just to teach biblical truth, but to embody it through active support, mentorship, and pastoral care.

For those struggling with trauma—especially ministers—healing begins when we shift our focus from the storm to the Savior. Storms rage and waves will rise. But as long as we keep our eyes on Jesus, we will not sink.

Dr. Oliver McMahan's *A Caring Church* (1999) and my own research both point to the importance of shifting focus in times of crisis. Trauma, when magnified, becomes the filter through which we see everything—our identity, our ministry, and even God. But healing happens when we recongnize Christ is greater than our struggles.

The Church must take an active role in providing ministers with a framework for healing, ensuring that no leader walks through suffering alone. When problems seem super-sized, the answer is not to minimize them but to maximize the presence of God.

To the minister struggling with trauma, your calling is not over. To the believer battling overwhelming pain, your story is not finished.

Where is your focus today?

Are you magnifying the storm or the Savior?

Reflection Questions for Chapter 2

Personal Reflection on Magnification and Perspective

1. Have you ever experienced a time when a personal struggle or failure seemed bigger than it actually was? How did your focus impact your emotions and ability to move forward?

2. McMahan & Hughes (1996) state that a lack of a caring community can make trauma feel worse. Have you ever felt alone in your pain? How did that isolation affect your ability to heal? In what ways do you tend to magnify your struggles? Do you find yourself replaying past failures, overanalyzing situations, or dwelling on what you cannot change?

Spiritual and Biblical Reflection

3. Matthew 14:22-33 tells the story of Peter walking on water. When he kept his eyes on Jesus, he was able to do the impossible, but when he focused on the storm, he began to sink. How does this passage relate to your own struggles?

4. Paul describes in 2 Corinthians 12:9 that God's strength is made perfect in weakness. How does this verse challenge the way you view your own limitations and failures?

5. Psalm 46:1 declares that "God is our refuge and strength, a very present help in trouble." How can you shift your focus from your problems to God's presence in your life?

Healing and Moving Forward

6. Dr. Taylor's research on ministers with trauma (2023) found that focusing on wounds rather than healing prevents recovery. What is one area of your life where you have been dwelling on past hurt rather than seeking healing?

7. Super-sizing problems is one of the enemy's greatest tactics to keep us discouraged (John 10:10). What lies have you believed about your struggles, and how can you replace them with God's truth?

8. If your problems feel overwhelming right now, what practical steps can you take to redirect your focus onto Christ? What role can prayer, Scripture, and community play in that process?

3

MONOPOLIZED

Misery loves company & sometimes he throws a party inviting all his negative friends.

Trauma has a way of monopolizing the mind. It traps us in cycles of negativity, rewiring how we think, feel, and respond to life. When we experience deep wounds—whether from personal loss, ministry burnout, or church hurt—our pain often becomes the lens through which we see everything. Instead of processing pain in a healthy way, we ruminate. We dwell. We relive. And soon, suffering becomes our identity.

In *The Practicing Way,* John Mark Comer (2024) highlights the power of intentional spiritual disciplines in reclaiming the mind from negativity and distraction. He argues that our minds, when left unchecked, will naturally drift toward self-defeating narratives, anxiety, and despair. The modern world, filled with noise and endless distractions, creates an environment where negative thoughts thrive, trapping people in cycles of emotional and spiritual exhaustion. Comer explains that the key to breaking this cycle is not passive avoidance but intentional redirection—learning to cultivate mental resilience through spiritual practices like silence, solitude, prayer, and community.

This concept is especially relevant for those navigating trauma and ministry burnout. When trauma monopolizes our minds, it convinces us that we are alone, beyond healing, and incapable of moving forward. Comer (2024) emphasizes that true healing begins when we disrupt these thought patterns by actively engaging in spiritual practices that draw us back to God's presence and truth.

In the same way, this chapter explores how trauma creates a cycle of negativity, isolates us, and distorts our perspective. Using biblical wisdom, psychological insights, and trauma-informed ministry approaches, we will examine how leaders, especially those wounded by church hurt, can shift from dwelling in suffering to embracing healing.

Similarly, Richard Foster's *Celebration of Discipline* (2018) explores how spiritual disciplines act as a counterbalance to trauma's grip on our lives. Foster highlights that solitude and confession, in particular, are powerful tools for breaking the chains of emotional and spiritual isolation. Trauma often isolates us by convincing us that no one understands our pain and that our suffering is too great to be shared.

However, Foster (2018) argues that solitude provides space for God's healing presence, while confession fosters community and accountability, ensuring that we do not bear our burdens alone. He writes, "The grace of God is mediated through the people of God… to receive healing, we must be willing to enter into honest confession."

For those struggling with church hurt, ministry trauma, or deep wounds of betrayal, Foster's insights are a reminder that healing is not a passive process—it requires stepping into intentional spiritual disciplines that create space for transformation. When trauma monopolizes our thoughts, we must choose to interrupt the cycle through practices that redirect our focus back to Christ.

The Isolation Trap: How Trauma Creates a Cycle of Negativity

One of the most deceptive aspects of trauma is that it convinces us we are alone. It whispers that no one understands that no one cares, and that reaching out will only lead to more pain. Isolation feels like protection—but it's actually a prison.

Elijah experienced this firsthand in 1 Kings 19:1-18. After a great spiritual victory, where God displayed His power against the prophets of Baal, Elijah should have been walking in confidence. Instead, he was running in fear. Queen Jezebel's threats overwhelmed him, and he fled into the wilderness alone.

Under the juniper tree, Elijah was completely overtaken by despair. He told God, "It is enough; now, O Lord, take my life, for I am no better than my fathers" (1 Kings 19:4, ESV). His trauma monopolized his thinking—convincing him that his work was meaningless, his future was over, and his life was worthless. This is how trauma works. It isolates. It magnifies. It distorts reality.

Instead of rebuking Elijah, God met him in his despair. He provided rest, nourishment, and reassurance. God showed Elijah that he was not alone—there were still 7,000 others in Israel who had not bowed to Baal. In other words, his pain was real, but his isolation was a lie.

McMahan (1995) in *Scriptural Counseling* explains that one of the biggest barriers to healing is believing that our suffering must be endured in solitude. He emphasizes that Scripture repeatedly points to healing in community.

Trauma thrives in silence and secrecy, but it loses power when we bring it into the light.

The Influence of Negative Thoughts: Depression, Self-Pity, and Bitterness

When trauma takes root, it does more than just wound us in the moment—it begins to shape how we think about ourselves, others, and even God. Over time, these distorted thoughts can take over, monopolizing the mind so that every experience, relationship, and opportunity is filtered through the lens of suffering rather than healing. Instead of seeing possibilities for restoration, we anticipate rejection. Instead of recognizing God's faithfulness, we focus on what was lost. Instead of stepping forward in faith, we retreat into a mindset dominated by fear, regret, and pain.

This pattern is exactly what the enemy desires. The Apostle Paul, understanding the dangers of unchecked thought patterns, urged believers, "Do not be conformed to this world, but be transformed by the renewal of your mind" (Romans 12:2). Renewal is not just about changing behavior—it is about changing the way we think. If we do not allow God to reshape our thinking, trauma fills the void. The longer we dwell in the pain, the deeper its grip becomes, leading to emotional and spiritual strongholds that feel impossible to break.

One of the most common effects of trauma is depression, where hopelessness begins to take root. When pain is left unprocessed, it clouds our vision of the future, convincing us that healing is unattainable. What once brought joy now feels meaningless, and the thought of moving forward seems impossible. Trauma whispers that our best days are behind us and that we are stuck in a cycle of suffering with no way out.

Closely tied to depression is self-pity, which keeps us locked in a victim mindset. While it is normal to grieve and acknowledge pain, self-pity convinces us that we are powerless to heal. It rewrites our identity, making suffering our defining characteristic rather than a chapter in our story. Instead of looking for ways to heal, we resign ourselves to believing that we will always be broken. But God never intended for us to remain in this state. He calls us out of despair and into His restoration, reminding us that while suffering is real, it does not have to be our permanent reality.

Perhaps one of the most dangerous results of unhealed trauma is bitterness. Hebrews 12:15 (ESV) warns, "See to it that no one fails to obtain the grace of God; that no 'root of bitterness' springs up and causes trouble, and by it many become defiled." Bitterness does not stay contained within our hearts—it spreads, poisoning our relationships, ministries, and faith. It creates walls between us and God, making it difficult to trust Him again. It also isolates us from others, as we struggle to let go of the pain inflicted by people who may have hurt us deeply.

Bitterness disguises itself as self-protection, convincing us that holding onto anger will prevent us from being hurt again. But in reality, bitterness does not protect—it destroys. It keeps us tied to past wounds, replaying them over and over instead of allowing God to bring healing. It does not bring justice, nor does it give us control. Instead, it robs us of peace, joy, and the ability to embrace the new things God wants to do in our lives.

Breaking free from trauma's grip requires more than just time—it requires an intentional decision to surrender our thoughts to God. Healing begins when we recognize that our minds were never meant to be held captive by suffering. Instead of conforming to the patterns of pain, we must allow God to transform our thinking, restoring hope where trauma once dictated despair.

Breaking the Monopoly: How to Shift from Suffering to Healing

So how do we break free? How do we stop allowing trauma to control our thoughts? The answer is not avoidance, but intentional renewal. Paul's teaching in Romans 12:2 provides a roadmap for healing: Breaking free from trauma's grip requires rejecting the world's false narrative that pain defines us, that brokenness is permanent, and that wounds inflicted by others—especially within the church—are a valid reason to walk away from the faith. Scripture calls believers to resist this deception, holding onto the truth that God is in the business of redemption. No matter how deep the wounds, His power to heal and restore far exceeds the damage inflicted by life's hardships. Refusing to accept the world's view of suffering allows space for God's truth to take root, reminding us that He can bring beauty even from the most painful experiences.

Healing is a process that demands patience, spiritual discipline, and a willingness to allow God to work deeply within us. It does not happen overnight, nor is it a passive experience. Spiritual disciplines such as prayer, fasting, and solitude are not merely religious practices but transformative tools that create space for renewal. As Foster (2018) emphasizes, these disciplines allow believers to step away from the noise of pain and listen for God's voice, fostering an environment where true healing can begin.

A renewed mind is cultivated through daily commitment. As Comer (2024) explains, renewal is not a single moment of clarity but a lifelong practice of shifting focus from trauma to truth. Worship, Scripture, fasting, and godly community serve as safeguards against the overwhelming grip of suffering. These practices disrupt trauma's monopoly over our thinking, allowing God's presence to reshape our perceptions and strengthen our faith.

As believers seek healing, clarity about God's will becomes more evident. Trauma has a way of distorting perspective, making it difficult to trust that God still has a purpose for our lives. However, when the mind is renewed, faith replaces doubt, and suffering no longer dictates the future. Many who have walked through healing find that their greatest pain becomes their greatest testimony—a living witness of God's redemptive power. Through renewal, what once seemed like an end becomes a new beginning, proof that God can bring life out of even the darkest seasons.

Takeaway: Shifting from Dwelling on Suffering to Embracing Healing.

If trauma has monopolized your mind, know this: you are not alone, and this is not the end of your story. The weight of suffering can feel unbearable at times, convincing you that healing is out of reach, that your pain is too deep, or that your past disqualifies you from restoration. But Scripture tells a different story. Time and time again, we see God meeting His people in their lowest moments—not with condemnation, but with compassion. Like Elijah, who sat under the juniper tree in despair, believing his work had been meaningless, God does not shame us for our weariness, our doubts, or our brokenness. Instead, He calls us back to Himself, nourishing our souls, reminding us of our purpose, and equipping us to continue the journey ahead.

Healing begins with a choice. It is a decision to no longer allow trauma to dictate your identity. It is choosing to break the cycle of isolation, refusing to let shame and bitterness control your thoughts. It is replacing the lies of suffering with the truth of God's Word, allowing Him to renew your mind and restore your hope. Trauma tells you that you will never move beyond this moment, but healing tells you that God is not finished with you yet.

The storm will rage. The waves will rise. The voices of doubt will try to pull you under. But no storm is greater than the Savior who walks on water. No darkness is stronger than the One who spoke light into existence. If we keep our eyes on Jesus, we will not sink. If we hold fast to His promises, we will not be consumed. His grace is sufficient, His strength is made perfect in weakness, and His love is more powerful than any wound we carry.

So, the question is—what will you choose to magnify today? Will you focus on the weight of your pain, or will you shift your gaze to the One who holds your healing? Will you allow trauma to define your future, or will you trust that God's redemption is already unfolding in your life? Healing is not always immediate, but it is always possible. The choice to step into it is yours.

Reflection Questions for Chapter 3

Personal Reflection

1. Have you ever found yourself stuck in a cycle of negative thinking after experiencing deep pain? What emotions or thought patterns tend to monopolize your mind?

2. How has bitterness, self-pity, or depression impacted your relationships with others? Have you noticed these emotions influencing the way you interact with family, friends, or your church community?

3. Elijah, in 1 Kings 19, allowed fear and exhaustion to drive him into isolation. Have there been moments in your life where pain caused you to run rather than reach out for help?

Spiritual and Biblical Reflection

4. Hebrews 12:15 warns about the danger of bitterness: "See to it that no one fails to obtain the grace of God; that no 'root of bitterness' springs up and causes trouble." Have you ever seen bitterness take root in your own life or the lives of others? What were the effects?

5. In 1 Kings 19, Elijah's despair was met with God's provision, rest, and reassurance. How does this passage challenge your

understanding of how God responds to pain?

6. The enemy often magnifies our wounds, convincing us that we are beyond redemption. Read 2 Corinthians 10:5, which calls believers to "take every thought captive to obey Christ." What are some practical ways you can redirect your thoughts when trauma seeks to monopolize them?

Healing and Moving Forward

7. In The Practicing Way, Comer (2024) argues that healing requires intentional renewal. What spiritual disciplines—such as prayer, worship, community, or silence—can you incorporate into your daily life to shift your focus from suffering to healing?

8. Richard Foster (2018) emphasizes the power of confession in breaking isolation. Who in your life do you trust enough to share your struggles with? If no one comes to mind, what steps can you take to build healthy, supportive relationships?

4

OSTRACIZED

We become our worst enemy we've had when we imprison ourselves on a lonely island of doubt.

In *Hope After Church Hurt,* Joe Dobbins (2022) highlights a difficult reality—many believers, especially those wounded by the church, find themselves in self-imposed exile. Hurt by betrayal, judgment, or rejection, they withdraw, believing that isolation is safer than vulnerability. The pain of feeling abandoned or misunderstood by the very people who should embody Christ's love often leads to spiritual loneliness and deep emotional wounds.

This experience is especially true for those in ministry. As I found in my research on ministers and trauma, many pastors and church leaders suffer in silence, carrying burdens they feel they cannot share. The stigma surrounding mental health in the church only reinforces this loneliness, making leaders feel as though seeking help is a sign of weakness rather than faith.

McMahan's *Scriptural Counseling* (1995) underscores the danger of isolation, explaining that when individuals face trauma but lack a biblical framework for healing, they often retreat inward instead of seeking help. He argues that Scripture itself provides a model for breaking free from self-imposed exile—one that calls people out of shame, into community, and toward healing.

This chapter explores the dangers of self-imposed isolation, the need for breaking the silence on mental health in the church, and the biblical truth that God calls us out of exile and into His family.

Self-Imposed Isolation: How Shame & Guilt Keep Us From Reaching Out

One of the greatest ironies of trauma and pain is that even though healing happens in community, the first response for many is to withdraw. The weight of shame, guilt, or feelings of unworthiness convinces people to retreat into spiritual and emotional isolation.

Larry Crabb (2005), in *Connecting: Healing for Ourselves and Our Relationships,* describes this pattern as a false sense of self-protection. He explains that when people experience deep wounds—whether from church hurt, personal failures, or emotional trauma—they tend to believe that pulling away will keep them safe from further harm. However, this isolation only reinforces the wounds, leading to:

Spiritual disconnection is one of the most dangerous effects of trauma, creating a false belief that suffering distances us from God's love. When pain takes hold, it whispers lies that convince us we are unworthy, forgotten, or too broken for redemption. Instead of turning to God for comfort, we may withdraw, feeling ashamed or abandoned. This separation is not from God's side—He remains near to the brokenhearted (Psalm 34:18)—but from our own perception, making it difficult to receive His grace. The enemy thrives on this deception, seeking to isolate us from the very source of our healing.

Trauma also leads to relational breakdown, making it difficult to trust others. When betrayal, rejection, or hurt originates from people we once relied on—especially within the church—it reinforces the belief that relationships are unsafe. The fear of being wounded again often causes individuals to build walls around their hearts, avoiding meaningful connections to protect themselves from further pain. However, this self-imposed isolation only deepens the loneliness, keeping them from the supportive community God designed for healing. While trust takes time to rebuild, avoiding relationships altogether prevents the very restoration we long for.

Emotional suppression compounds these struggles, as unprocessed pain does not disappear—it festers. Rather than acknowledging hurt, many people push their emotions inward, believing that ignoring them will make them go away. Yet, bottled-up pain eventually manifests in other ways, leading to anxiety, depression, or physical exhaustion. God did not create us to carry our burdens alone. Scripture encourages believers to "cast all your anxieties on Him, because He cares for you" (1 Peter 5:7, NIV). Healing begins when we stop suppressing pain and allow God and trusted individuals into our struggles, embracing the process of restoration rather than avoiding it.

In my research, I found that many ministers suffering from burnout or betrayal did not leave ministry because they lacked faith, but because they felt abandoned. Rather than facing judgment or pity, they withdrew into silence, believing no one would understand. But self-imposed exile never leads to healing. In fact, it only deepens the wounds.

The Stigma of Mental Health in the Church: Breaking the Silence on Depression and Faith

One of the greatest reasons so many believers and leaders remain in isolation is the stigma surrounding mental health in the church. For decades, many within Christian communities have misunderstood mental health struggles, equating depression, anxiety, or trauma with a lack of faith. While faith in Christ does bring healing, it does not mean believers are immune to suffering.

McMahan (1995) explains that scriptural counseling must take a balanced approach, recognizing that far too long, the church has struggled to properly address mental health, often equating struggles with faithlessness or spiritual weakness. Many believers, particularly those in ministry, have felt the weight of this misunderstanding. They have been led to believe that their battles with depression, anxiety, or trauma are a sign that they lack trust in God or that they simply need to pray harder. However, Scripture does not support this view. Throughout the Bible, we see faithful men and women—Elijah, David, Job, and even the Apostle Paul—wrestling with deep sorrow, fear, and emotional suffering. Their struggles did not disqualify them; instead, God met them in their pain, offering strength, renewal, and healing. Mental health struggles are not always spiritual failures; they are part of the human experience, and God's grace is sufficient even in our weakest moments.

Depression and anxiety are real battles, even for the strongest believers. Just as physical illnesses affect the body, mental health challenges can weigh heavily on the mind and soul. David, a man after God's own heart, wrote countless psalms of lament, crying out to God in seasons of despair. Elijah, after a great spiritual victory, withdrew into isolation, asking God to take his life. Even Jesus, in the

Garden of Gethsemane, experienced such intense anguish that He sweat drops of blood. These examples remind us that experiencing emotional distress is not an indication of a lack of faith—it is a reality that even the most devoted followers of Christ have faced. The good news is that God does not abandon us in our struggles; He draws near to the brokenhearted and saves those crushed in spirit (Psalm 34:18).

One of the greatest obstacles to healing is the stigma that still surrounds seeking help within Christian communities. Many believers suffer in silence, afraid that admitting their struggles will lead to judgment or rejection. But seeking help—whether through counseling, pastoral care, or community support—is not a lack of faith. It is an act of wisdom. Proverbs 11:14 (NLT) tells us that "Without wise leadership, a nation falls; there is safety in having many advisers." God designed us for community, to bear one another's burdens and to walk through trials together. Isolation only deepens the wounds of trauma, but reaching out for help creates space for healing. Whether through professional Christian counseling, support groups, or trusted mentors, seeking help is a tangible step toward embracing God's restoration.

Breaking free from the chains of isolation and stigma requires a shift in perspective. The church must become a place of refuge, not rejection, for those battling mental health struggles. Leaders and congregants alike must challenge harmful narratives that suggest emotional pain is a sign of spiritual failure. Instead, we must create environments where people can be honest about their struggles, find support, and receive the healing that God longs to bring. Just as Jesus reached out and touched the untouchable—the lepers, the outcasts, the broken—He calls His church to do the same today. God does not leave us in our suffering; He walks with us through it, offering hope, restoration, and the promise that we are never alone.

Larry Crabb (2013) expands on this idea, arguing that true biblical community requires breaking the silence around mental health. He emphasizes that healing happens when people can bring their pain into the open, free from shame and judgment.

Dobbins (2022) agrees, stating that one of the biggest sources of church hurt is when believers feel their suffering is dismissed, invalidated, or overly spiritualized. Many people who have left the church did not leave because of doctrine but because they felt unseen and unheard in their pain.

I found that ministers are among the most vulnerable to this struggle. Many pastors battle depression and anxiety yet feel pressure to "stay strong" for others, rather than admitting their own need for help. The truth is mental health struggles do not make someone weak—they make them human. Jesus Himself experienced deep emotional pain, weeping openly (John 11:35) and sweating drops of blood in distress (Luke 22:44). The Bible never portrays suffering as a sign of failure; rather, it shows that God meets us in our suffering.

The Leper Healed by Jesus (Luke 17:11-19)

One of the most powerful biblical examples of breaking free from isolation is found in Luke 17:11-19, where Jesus heals ten lepers. In biblical times, lepers were the ultimate outcasts. They were forbidden from entering cities, required to call out "Unclean! Unclean!" when approaching others, and often lived in total isolation. Society saw them as beyond hope—permanently ostracized. Yet in Luke 17,

Jesus does what no one else would—He sees them, speaks to them, and heals them.

One of the most profound truths about Jesus' ministry is that He meets the outcast where they are. In Luke 17:11-19, the ten lepers did not have to cleanse themselves before approaching Him. Society had cast them aside, labeling them as unclean, yet Jesus did not demand that they be healed before He acknowledged them. He saw them in their suffering, heard their cries for mercy, and responded with compassion. This is the heart of the gospel—God does not wait for us to be whole before He welcomes us into His presence. He meets us in the rawness of our pain, in the midst of our brokenness, and extends His healing grace. Many who have experienced church hurt or ministry wounds often feel like spiritual lepers, unworthy of restoration. But just as Jesus reached out to those whom society rejected, He reaches out to us, reminding us that our wounds do not disqualify us from His love.

However, healing is not just about being seen—it also requires stepping out of isolation. When Jesus told the lepers to "Go, show yourselves to the priests" (Luke 17:14, ESV), He was instructing them to take a step of faith before they even saw their healing take place. In Jewish tradition, lepers were required to be declared clean by the priests before re-entering society. By commanding them to go, Jesus was restoring them not just physically, but socially and spiritually. True healing is not just about personal restoration; it is about reconnecting with the body of Christ, stepping back into community, and refusing to let trauma keep us in solitude. Many who have been hurt by the church choose to withdraw rather than risk being wounded again. But just as the lepers had to walk toward restoration, we too must take intentional steps toward healing.

God calls us out of hiding and into His family, where we can find belonging and support in the right community.

The final lesson from this passage is the transformative power of gratitude. Out of the ten lepers who were healed, only one returned to Jesus to offer thanks. While all ten experienced God's grace, only one fully embraced the relationship it offered. This highlights an important truth—healing is more than just physical or emotional restoration; it is a spiritual transformation that comes through worship and gratitude. Too often, we focus on what we need from God and forget to acknowledge what He has already done. Gratitude shifts our perspective from our suffering to His goodness. It keeps our hearts tender rather than bitter. When we choose to thank God for His faithfulness, even in the midst of our struggles, we step into deeper healing that is not just about relief from pain but about renewal of the soul. True wholeness comes not just when our wounds are healed, but when our hearts are restored to worship.

Healing is more than the absence of pain—it is the presence of God. Psalm 22:3 tells us that God inhabits the praises of His people, meaning that when we lift our voices in worship, we create a space where His presence dwells. Worship is not just a response to healing; it is the pathway to it. When we praise God, even in the midst of our brokenness, we invite His Spirit to move in our lives. The act of worship shifts our focus from our suffering to our Savior, from our wounds to His worthiness. It declares that our pain does not define us—His presence does. In the darkest seasons, when trauma seeks to monopolize our thoughts, worship becomes the breakthrough that realigns our hearts with the truth of who God is. Worship does not ignore our wounds, but it refuses to let them have the final word.

Where the Spirit of the Lord is, there is liberty (2

Corinthians 3:17, NKJV). Worship creates an atmosphere for freedom. Many people wait to worship until they feel whole again, but true freedom is found in worshiping through the process. Trauma has a way of shackling us in fear, doubt, and isolation, convincing us that we must fix ourselves before we can come before God. But in reality, worship is what breaks the chains.

In God's presence, the burdens we carry begin to lift, the lies we've believed are exposed, and the walls we've built around our hearts start to fall. True healing happens not just when our external wounds close, but when our spirits are awakened to the reality that we are fully known, fully loved, and fully free in His presence. Worship is more than a song—it is the key that unlocks the door to the wholeness God has always intended for us.

James reminds us in James 4:10 (NIV), "Humble yourselves before the Lord, and he will lift you up." True healing begins with humility—acknowledging that we cannot restore ourselves, but that God can. Trauma often tempts us to build walls of self-protection, convincing us that we must carry our burdens alone. Yet, James calls us to surrender, to lay down our pride, our pain, and even our need for control at the feet of Jesus. When we do, God does not leave us in our brokenness; He lifts us up. His lifting is not merely an escape from suffering but a restoration of purpose, dignity, and strength. In humbling ourselves before Him, we find that healing is not just about relief from pain—it is about being raised into the fullness of who He created us to be.

Takeaway: God Calls Us Out of Isolation and Into His Family.

Breaking free from trauma's grip requires an intentional and daily commitment to renewal. In 2 Corinthians 10:5, Paul reminds us to "take every thought captive to obey Christ." This passage highlights the importance of actively confronting the lies that trauma tells us—lies that say we are beyond healing, unworthy of love, or incapable of moving forward. Transformation does not happen by accident; it is an active process of surrendering our thoughts, our pain, and our perspective to God.

The world would have us believe that our trauma defines us, that our brokenness is permanent, and that the wounds inflicted by others—especially within the church—are a valid reason to walk away from the faith. But Scripture calls us to reject this false narrative. Just as Paul instructed the Corinthians to take control of their thoughts and align them with Christ's truth, we too must challenge the patterns of thinking that keep us trapped in cycles of despair. God's truth is greater than our suffering, and He calls us to step into a new way of thinking—one that does not allow pain to have the final say. By leaning into His promises, we shift our focus from what has been done to us toward what He is doing in us, and ultimately, toward the healing and purpose He has prepared for us.

Healing is not an overnight experience; it is a journey. Transformation requires patience, spiritual discipline, and an openness to let God do His work in us. Richard Foster (2018) emphasizes that spiritual disciplines are essential in this process, guiding us into practices like prayer, fasting, worship, and biblical meditation. These disciplines are not just religious exercises; they serve as anchors, grounding us when the weight of our past threatens to pull us under. When trauma monopolizes our thoughts, it creates an internal prison where fear, shame, and doubt keep us locked away from hope. But God invites us into a process of renewal, where our minds can be restored and our perspective reshaped by His truth.

Renewing the mind is not something that happens once and for all; it is a daily decision to shift our focus from the past to God's promises. John Mark Comer (2024) explains that what fills our minds ultimately shapes our lives. If we fixate on pain, betrayal, or self-doubt, those thoughts will dictate our actions, reinforcing the cycle of trauma. But when we choose to immerse ourselves in God's Word, in worship, and in godly community, our thinking begins to change. Spiritual disciplines act as a disruption to trauma's monopoly, forcing us to step outside of destructive thought patterns and realign with God's plan for our lives.

One of the greatest struggles of trauma is that it distorts our ability to see God's will clearly. Pain has a way of clouding our vision, convincing us that the suffering we have endured is the end of our story. But Paul reminds us that when our minds are renewed, we gain clarity about God's purpose. Many ministers and believers who have walked through deep pain have later realized that their greatest struggles became their most powerful testimonies. The very thing that once felt like a death sentence was what God used to bring healing to others. Renewal does not erase the past, but it reframes it—revealing that even in suffering, God is still writing a story of redemption. It is in the renewing of our minds that we come to see that God never wastes our pain but transforms it into something far greater than we ever imagined.

You Are Not Alone

If you have been wounded by the church. If you have withdrawn in shame. If you believe your pain has made you unworthy of love. I know what that feels like. I have walked through the kind of pain that makes you want to disappear, to pull away from everyone and everything that once felt safe. I have experienced the sting of betrayal, the deafening silence after broken relationships, and the overwhelming weight of wondering if I would ever feel whole again.

There was a time when I believed I was beyond redemption. That the mistakes I made, the hurt I endured, and the loneliness I carried had somehow placed me beyond God's reach. I thought isolation was the only way to protect myself from more pain. But in that loneliness, in that self-imposed exile, I discovered something I had forgotten:

God sees you.

Not the version of you that tries to put on a strong face. Not the you that hides behind ministry, performance, or pretending everything is okay. He sees the real you. The one who is hurting. The one who is tired. The one who wonders if there is anything left worth saving. And yet, even in that place of brokenness, He calls you by name.

The same Jesus who healed the lepers, who restored Elijah when he was ready to give up, and who comforted the brokenhearted has never stopped pursuing you. His love is not dependent on how strong you feel, how perfectly you perform, or how well you hide your pain. His love goes to the outcast, the weary, and the ones the world has given up on.

I know, because I was one of them.

But I also know this—isolation is not your home. God

is calling you out of the shadows, out of the pain that has kept you bound, and into His healing presence. He is offering more than just survival—He is offering restoration, hope, and purpose beyond what you can see right now.

I won't pretend it's easy. Saying "yes" to healing means stepping out of the familiar, even if the familiar is painful. It means trusting that God is still good, even when people have let you down. It means believing that you are still worthy of love, grace, and a future.

I've been there. And I can tell you this—there is life after pain. There is hope after church hurt. There is healing after heartbreak.

The only question is—will you let Him heal you?

Reflection Questions for Chapter 4

Personal Reflection: Understanding Isolation and Its Impact

1 Have you ever found yourself withdrawing from relationships, community, or even God due to hurt, guilt, or shame? What emotions led you to retreat?

2 Dobbins (2022) argues that the church often unintentionally pushes wounded people into further isolation by not acknowledging their pain. Have you ever felt unseen or dismissed by a faith community when you were struggling? What impact did that have on your faith?

Spiritual & Biblical Reflection: Breaking the Stigma of Mental and Emotional Struggles

3 Have you ever felt that struggling with mental health—whether depression, anxiety, or trauma—was a sign of weak faith? Where did that belief come from?

4 Jesus Himself experienced deep sorrow (John 11:35) and distress (Luke 22:44). How does knowing that Jesus understands emotional pain challenge the stigma around mental health in the church?

Healing and Moving Forward: Stepping Out of Isolation

5 What fears or doubts keep you from seeking help or community? Do you fear rejection, judgment, or being misunderstood? How have those fears influenced your decisions?

5

TRIVIALIZED

Why is it that many of our friends find less value in what we've been through than we do?

I remember the moment when I finally mustered up the courage to share my pain with someone I thought would understand. I sat across the table, heart pounding, as I opened up about the trauma I had been carrying. I didn't need solutions or even sympathy—I just needed someone to acknowledge that what I had been through was real. Instead, what I received was a casual shrug and a dismissive response: "Well, at least it's not as bad as what some people go through."

It was like a punch to the gut. I had poured out my soul, hoping for validation, but instead, my pain was measured against some invisible scale of suffering. My friend meant no harm, but their words minimized the very real wounds I was trying to process. I left that conversation feeling more alone than before, questioning whether my pain even mattered. Had I been overreacting? Was I making too much of my own suffering?

This experience was not unique. Over the years, I have

learned that one of the most painful aspects of trauma is not just what happened to us—but how others respond to it. When our pain is minimized, dismissed, or compared to someone else's, it can deepen the wounds we are already trying to heal. We begin to wonder if we are weak for struggling, if we should "just get over it," or if our experiences are too insignificant to warrant true support.

The Pain of Being Misunderstood: When Others Minimize Our Suffering

There are few wounds as painful as opening up about deep suffering, only to have it dismissed, minimized, or met with indifference. Trauma is already isolating in itself, but when those around us fail to recognize the weight of our suffering, it compounds the pain, making us feel unseen and unheard. Dr. Henry Cloud and Dr. John Townsend, in *Safe People* (1995), discuss how many individuals struggle to provide meaningful support because they lack the emotional capacity to sit with someone in pain. Instead of offering true empathy, they resort to avoidance, oversimplification, or even judgment.

This tendency to downplay suffering often comes from discomfort rather than cruelty. Many people do not know how to engage with another's pain, so they attempt to rationalize it or offer a quick fix. Instead of validating a person's experience, they might say, "At least it wasn't worse," or, "You should be grateful for what you still have." While these statements may be well-intended, they fail to acknowledge the depth of someone's suffering. Dr. Cloud, in *Changes That Heal* (1992), emphasizes that true healing begins with recognition—both from within and from others. Without it, those who are wounded may feel forced to suppress their pain rather than work through it.

The problem of being misunderstood is especially painful for those in ministry. Pastors, counselors, and leaders often find that their trauma is minimized because of the expectation that they should be resilient. Others assume that their faith should be enough to sustain them, without recognizing that even the strongest believers need care and understanding. Brené Brown, though not a Christian author, speaks powerfully about vulnerability in *Daring Greatly* (2012), explaining that when someone's pain is met with dismissal rather than empathy, they often retreat further into isolation, feeling that no one is truly willing to carry their burden with them.

Scripture reminds us that God does not treat our suffering lightly. He does not brush aside our pain with quick solutions or call us to simply "get over it." Instead, He meets us with compassion, reminding us that He sees and understands every hardship we endure. Psalm 34:18 (ESV) declares, "The Lord is near to the brokenhearted and saves the crushed in spirit." When others fail to validate our suffering, God does not. And that is where our healing begins.

The Church's Response to Trauma: Misguided Platitudes vs. Genuine Support

The church is meant to be a place of refuge, yet for many, it has been a source of deeper wounds. While the body of Christ is called to "bear one another's burdens" (Galatians 6:2, NKJV), too often, trauma survivors are met with responses that minimize their pain rather than affirm their suffering. This dismissal can take many forms—well-intentioned but unhelpful spiritual platitudes, avoidance of difficult conversations, or the expectation that healing should follow a specific timeline.

Dr. John Townsend, in *People Fuel* (2019), explains

that one of the biggest relational failures in the church is the tendency to offer solutions when what people truly need is presence. Many Christians respond to trauma by offering trite answers like "Everything happens for a reason," or "You just need to trust God more." While faith is indeed central to healing, these phrases can unintentionally invalidate the pain someone is experiencing. Townsend argues that biblical community requires more than just words—it requires action. Genuine support means sitting with people in their pain, listening without judgment, and resisting the urge to fix what only God can heal.

Cloud and Townsend, in *Boundaries* (1992), highlights another issue that often arises in the church: the expectation that Christians must always be strong. Many believers feel pressure to suppress their pain for fear of being seen as lacking faith. This often leads to a cycle of denial rather than healing. The reality is that even the strongest men and women in Scripture—David, Elijah, Job—experienced deep suffering, questioned God, and wrestled with their emotions. The church should be a place where these struggles are acknowledged, not silenced.

True biblical support does not minimize suffering; it engages with it. It acknowledges the depth of trauma while pointing toward hope. It does not rush people toward healing but walks with them in the process. When the church learns to embrace pain rather than avoid it, it becomes the refuge that Christ intended it to be.

Dealing with Pain, Grief, and Unmet Expectations

Suffering often carries with it a silent question: Why is this happening to me? When we experience trauma, grief, or disappointment, we naturally seek answers, but the responses we receive—especially from well-meaning friends, family, or even the church—often leave us feeling more frustrated than comforted. We long for someone to acknowledge the depth of our pain, but instead, we are met with dismissive phrases like "Everything happens for a reason," "God won't give you more than you can handle," or "You just need to trust God more." While these statements may be intended to offer encouragement, they often come across as minimizing the real struggle of suffering.

Timothy Keller, in *Walking with God through Pain and Suffering* (2013), argues that many Christians have a deficient understanding of suffering because they expect faith to act as a shield against hardship. When suffering inevitably comes, it is often met with shallow theology—platitudes that seek to bypass grief rather than walk through it. Keller reminds us that throughout Scripture, God does not ask people to ignore their pain, but rather, He walks with them in it. He does not always provide immediate relief, but He assures His presence. The Christian faith does not promise a life free from suffering, but it does promise that God is near to the brokenhearted (Psalm 34:18). Understanding this allows us to approach our pain with honesty, rather than feeling pressured to suppress it in order to meet religious expectations.

Lysa TerKeurst, in I*t's Not Supposed to Be This Way* (2018), speaks candidly about the pain of unmet expectations. Many believers are raised to believe that if they follow God faithfully, life will unfold in predictable and pleasant ways. When life takes an unexpected and painful turn, they are left wrestling with disappointment, confusion, and even feelings of betrayal. People often respond by trying to explain away suffering, as though wrapping it in a neat theological bow will make it hurt less. But TerKeurst emphasizes that true faith is not about having all the answers—it is about trusting that God is still present even in the midst of suffering. She encourages believers to embrace the reality that things are not supposed to be this way because we live in a fallen world. But even when life is broken, God is still writing a redemptive story.

Larry Crabb, in *Shattered Dreams: God's Unexpected Path to Joy* (2001), builds on this idea by showing how suffering, rather than being an obstacle to faith, can actually be the very thing that deepens it. He suggests that when our dreams are shattered, we are given an opportunity to reevaluate our trust in God. Too often, people expect others to validate their pain, but when validation does not come—or when others minimize their suffering—they feel even more isolated. Crabb argues that instead of seeking affirmation from others, we must learn to bring our pain directly to God. He does not dismiss it or rush past it, but He allows it to refine us, drawing us closer to Him. True healing does not come from receiving the right words from people; it comes from allowing God to use our suffering to shape us into who He has called us to be.

Esther Fleece Allen, in *No More Faking Fine: Ending the Pretending* (2017), echoes this by emphasizing the power of lament. The church often struggles with the concept of lament, favoring messages of victory and joy over honest expressions of grief. As a result, many Christians feel they must suppress their pain in order to appear spiritually strong. Allen argues that this is both unhealthy and unbiblical. Scripture is filled with laments—from the cries of Job and David to the anguish of Jesus in the Garden of Gethsemane. God invites His people to bring their raw, unfiltered emotions to Him. Lament is not faithlessness—it is an act of deep trust, recognizing that God is big enough to handle our deepest pain. Healing begins not when we pretend everything is fine, but when we stop faking fine and allow ourselves to grieve in the presence of a loving God.

Taken together, these perspectives reveal an important truth: suffering is not something to be trivialized, dismissed, or explained away. It is something to be acknowledged, processed, and ultimately surrendered to God. When others fail to validate our pain, we must remember that God sees every tear, hears every cry, and is present in every moment of grief. True healing is found not in human explanations, but in the presence of a God who walks with us through every sorrow.

Job's Friends and Their Failure to Comfort (Job 2:11-13)

The story of Job provides one of the most profound lessons on how not to respond to someone's suffering. Job endured unimaginable loss—his wealth, his health, and worst of all, his children. In his grief, he longed for comfort, for someone to acknowledge the depths of his sorrow. At first, his friends seemed to understand. Job 2:11-13 describes how they came to him, wept with him, and sat in silence for seven days. In this moment, they did exactly what Job needed—they simply showed up.

But then they started speaking.

Rather than offering empathy, Job's friends began to analyze his suffering, insisting that he must have done something to deserve it. They trivialized his grief by turning it into a theological argument, failing to recognize that what he needed was not explanations, but presence. Dr. Dan Allender, in *The Healing Path* (1999), explains that one of the biggest mistakes we make when engaging with another's pain is trying to interpret their suffering rather than simply acknowledging it. Job's friends got it right when they sat in silence, but they lost sight of compassion when they tried to explain his suffering instead of walking through it with him.

The failure of Job's friends is a warning to all of us. Sometimes, the best way to support someone is not to offer answers but to sit with them in their pain. True comfort is found not in trying to fix someone's suffering, but in reminding them that they are not alone.

Takeaway: Finding Validation and Comfort in God, Not People.

Perhaps the hardest but most necessary lesson in healing is this: our validation does not come from people. No matter how much we long for others to recognize our pain, the truth is that some never will. Some will minimize our suffering. Some will misunderstand. Some will walk away when we need them most.

But God does not.

Dr. Henry Cloud, in *Changes That Heal*, reminds us that people can only offer what they are capable of giving. Some individuals, no matter how much we wish otherwise, do not have the emotional depth to meet us where we are. If we place our entire sense of worth and healing in their hands, we will be continually disappointed. Instead, we must turn to the One who never trivializes our suffering—God Himself.

Psalm 56:8 tells us that God collects every tear we cry. He does not dismiss our grief. He does not rush us through healing. He does not compare our pain to others. He takes it seriously, even when people do not. And it is in Him—not in human validation—that we find true comfort.

Healing begins when we stop waiting for others to understand and accept that God already does. He sees what we have been through. He knows the depth of our wounds. And He promises that He will be the One to restore us.

So, if you have been dismissed, if your suffering has been minimized, if you have been told to "just get over it" when your heart is still breaking—take heart. God sees it all. He has never trivialized your pain, and He never will. The question is not whether people will validate your suffering—the question is whether you will trust that God already has.

Reflection Questions for Chapter 5

Personal Reflection

1. Have you ever experienced a time when someone minimized your pain or dismissed your suffering? How did their response impact your healing process, and how did you internalize their words?

2. In what ways have you struggled with the need for validation from others regarding your trauma? How has this desire influenced your ability to process your pain in a healthy way?

Spiritual and Biblical Reflection

3. Job's friends initially sat with him in silence but later tried to explain away his suffering (Job 2:11-13). How does their response compare to how you have seen others respond to trauma—either in your life or in the church? What can we learn from their failure?

4. Psalm 56:8 says that God collects every tear we cry. How does this verse challenge the idea that suffering must be validated by people in order to be significant? How does it shape your understanding of God's care for you in times of pain?

Healing and Moving Forward

5. How can you shift your focus from seeking validation from others to finding comfort in God? What practical steps can you take to release the need for external affirmation and rest in God's understanding?

6. How can you be a source of true support for others who are suffering? Reflect on the difference between offering quick fixes and being a presence in someone's pain. What changes can you make in how you respond to those who are hurting?

6

CATEGORIZED

It is time to call our suffering what it is and say, "It is written" to the categories of pain we've found ourselves in.

I remember a season in my life when I couldn't even name what I was going through. I knew I was hurting, but I didn't know how to define it. Was it grief? Was it betrayal? Was it exhaustion? It was all of those things, yet none of those labels seemed to fully capture the weight I carried. I felt stuck in a fog, unable to process my pain because I had no framework to place it in. Instead of dealing with it, I did what many people do—I pushed through, pretending I was fine, hoping that time alone would bring healing.

But time didn't fix it. The pain followed me, showing up in unexpected ways. I would find myself irritable over small things, withdrawing from people I loved, or sitting in church feeling completely disconnected from God. It wasn't until someone looked me in the eye and said, "Call it what it is," that I realized I had been avoiding the very thing I needed to confront. That moment was a turning point. Naming my suffering didn't make it disappear, but it did give me power over it. It allowed me to bring it to God with clarity instead of confusion.

Many people walk through life carrying unnamed wounds. They feel the weight of their experiences, but they struggle to categorize their pain in a way that makes healing possible. That's why this chapter is so important. It is time to call our suffering what it is and say, "It is written" over the categories of pain we find ourselves in. It is time to recognize the lies trauma has told us and replace them with the truth of God's Word. Until we do, we will continue to let our pain define us instead of allowing God to redefine our pain for His purpose.

Naming the Pain: Identifying and Acknowledging Different Types of Trauma

Trauma is not a one-size-fits-all experience. What wounds one person deeply may not affect another in the same way, and yet, all trauma leaves its mark. Some wounds are visible, like a soldier returning from war with PTSD, while others are hidden beneath the surface, such as the emotional scars of childhood neglect. Recognizing and naming trauma is the first step toward healing because we cannot heal what we refuse to acknowledge.

In psychotherapy, trauma is often categorized into different types, each with distinct emotional, cognitive, and physiological effects. Acute trauma refers to a single, distressing event—a car accident, a violent attack, or an unexpected loss. The suddenness of acute trauma can leave an individual in a state of shock, struggling with intrusive thoughts, hypervigilance, or difficulty processing what has occurred. Chronic trauma, on the other hand, develops over time. This includes experiences like prolonged emotional abuse, ongoing neglect, or persistent exposure to unsafe environments. Chronic trauma often rewires the brain's stress response, leading to long-term struggles with anxiety, depression, and difficulty trusting others.

Then there is complex trauma, which occurs when multiple traumatic events layers on top of one another, often beginning in childhood. This type of trauma can stem from repeated betrayal, sustained emotional or physical abuse, or long-term exposure to dysfunctional relationships. It often results in deep-seated feelings of worthlessness, struggles with self-regulation, and a distorted sense of identity. Complex trauma can also influence how an individual sees God—many struggle to trust Him if their primary caregivers were unreliable or abusive.

From a clinical perspective, understanding the nature of trauma allows for more effective interventions. Cognitive Behavioral Therapy (CBT) helps individuals reframe distorted thinking patterns that trauma reinforces—such as the belief that they are always in danger or that they are unworthy of love. Eye Movement Desensitization and Reprocessing (EMDR) has been particularly useful in treating post-traumatic stress, allowing individuals to reprocess distressing memories so that they no longer hold the same emotional intensity. Trauma-Focused Cognitive Behavioral Therapy (TF-CBT) is widely used for those who experienced childhood trauma, helping them integrate painful memories into a cohesive narrative that allows for healing.

Spiritually, naming trauma is equally critical. Scripture repeatedly shows us that healing begins with confession—not just of sin, but of suffering. David, in Psalm 22, cries out to God in his distress, naming his pain rather than suppressing it. Jesus Himself acknowledged His anguish in the Garden of Gethsemane, showing that even the Son of God did not dismiss the weight of His suffering. Naming our pain does not mean dwelling on it, but rather recognizing it so that it can be surrendered to God.

Unacknowledged trauma often leads to avoidant coping mechanisms—numbing through workaholism, addiction, or spiritual bypassing, where people use religious language to cover up deep wounds rather than address them. But healing requires a willingness to say, "This happened to me, and it hurt." It requires sitting with the discomfort long enough to bring it into God's presence, where true restoration can take place.

Many people hesitate to name their pain because they fear it will consume them, but the opposite is true. What remains unnamed remains in control. By identifying and categorizing trauma, we take the first step toward reclaiming our narratives. As Dr. McMahan writes in *Becoming a Shepherd,* "A shepherd does not ignore the wounds of the flock; he binds them." We must do the same with ourselves—naming the wounds, acknowledging the depth of our suffering, and allowing the Great Shepherd to begin the work of healing.

For those who have lived in survival mode for so long that they have forgotten how to process their suffering, this step will not be easy. It takes courage to call pain by its name, to admit that we have been wounded in ways we may not fully understand. But when we do, we begin to loosen the grip that trauma has had on our lives. We move from being prisoners of our past to individuals on the path to wholeness. And that is where true transformation begins.

One of the greatest challenges in the healing journey is identifying and acknowledging the pain we have endured. Too often, suffering is left undefined, swept under the rug, or categorized in a way that minimizes its impact. But true healing requires clarity. If we do not name our pain, we cannot address it properly. In *Becoming a Shepherd,* McMahan (2005) highlights that shepherding people well—whether in ministry or in our own lives—requires an honest understanding of where they have been wounded. When trauma is left unexamined, it festers. But when it is brought into the light, it becomes a place where God's restoration can begin.

Again, trauma takes many forms. There is the deep wound of betrayal, the kind that leaves us questioning the very foundation of trust. There is the grief of loss, whether through death, divorce, or the end of a dream. Some experience abandonment, carrying the weight of being left behind by people who once promised to stay. Others endure spiritual abuse, where faith itself is weaponized against them, distorting the truth of God's love. And then there is the trauma of personal failure, where our own mistakes haunt us, convincing us that we are beyond redemption.

Jeffery A. Wilson, in *Evading Trouble* (2021), speaks to the reality that many people attempt to escape their pain rather than confront it. He explains that avoidance is a defense mechanism—a way to protect ourselves from reopening wounds. Yet, avoidance only delays the inevitable. When we refuse to categorize our pain, it remains unhealed, controlling us from beneath the surface. Wilson urges readers to acknowledge their suffering, not as a means of dwelling on it but as the first step toward overcoming it. Until we identify the categories of pain we have been placed in—whether by others, by circumstances, or by our own choices—we remain bound by them.

Speaking Truth Over Lies: Using Scripture to Combat Despair

One of the greatest deceptions of trauma is that it

distorts truth. It tells us that we are unworthy, that healing is impossible, that we are defined by what has happened to us. But as believers, we are called to speak truth over lies—to declare what is written in God's Word rather than accept the false narratives of our suffering.

In *Becoming a Shepherd*, McMahan (2005) emphasizes the power of truth in the healing process. Shepherds do not merely lead their sheep away from danger—they remind them of who they are and where they belong. Many who suffer trauma experience an identity crisis, believing that their pain is the final word on their story. But Scripture tells a different story.

Psalm 147:3 declares, "He heals the brokenhearted and binds up their wounds." Trauma tells us we will always be broken, but God's Word tells us we are being healed. Isaiah 61:3 speaks of beauty from ashes. The enemy whispers that our lives are beyond restoration, but Scripture proclaims that our suffering is never wasted. Romans 8:28 reminds us that "all things work together for good for those who love God." The world tells us that pain is pointless, but God promises redemption.

Lies thrive in silence, but truth flourishes when spoken. This is why we must actively declare God's promises over our lives. When despair tells us we will never recover, we respond, "It is written." When shame tells us we are beyond redemption, we counter, "It is written." When fear tells us that the past has stolen our future, we stand firm and say, "It is written." Healing begins when we replace the voice of trauma with the voice of truth.

Jesus Resisting Temptation in the Wilderness (Matthew 4:1-11) because, Jesus Himself, demonstrated the power of speaking truth over lies in the wilderness. In Matthew 4:1-11, He faced temptation from the enemy after forty days of fasting. The devil attempted to exploit His hunger, His vulnerability, and His divine mission. But rather than engaging with the enemy's deception, Jesus responded with Scripture. Each time Satan presented a lie, Jesus countered with "It is written."

This passage offers a profound lesson for those walking through suffering. Trauma functions much like the enemy's voice in the wilderness—it seeks to manipulate our weakness, convince us that God has abandoned us, and offer temporary solutions that do more harm than good. But Jesus showed us the way forward: we combat lies with truth.

Just as Jesus declared, "It is written," when faced with temptation, we must do the same when faced with the whispers of despair. When trauma tells us we are alone, we declare, "It is written, 'I will never leave you nor forsake you'" (Hebrews 13:5, NKJV). When suffering convinces us that God does not see our pain, we say, "It is written, 'The Lord is near to the brokenhearted'" (Psalm 34:18). When doubt tells us that our future is ruined, we proclaim, "It is written, 'For I know the plans I have for you, declares the Lord, plans to prosper you and not to harm you'" (Jeremiah 29:11).

The example of Jesus in the wilderness teaches us that truth is our greatest weapon against suffering. It is not enough to simply hope that the lies of trauma will fade away—we must actively combat them with the Word of God.

Takeaway: God's Word is the Key to Reframing Our Suffering.

At some point, every person who has suffered must make a choice: will they allow trauma to define them, or will they define their trauma in light of God's truth? The enemy would love nothing more than for us to remain trapped in the categories of pain we have experienced—believing that we are abandoned, beyond help, or permanently broken. But the moment we declare, "It is written," we reclaim our identity in Christ.

McMahan (2005) writes that a shepherd's role is not only to lead but to reframe—to help those in pain see themselves through the lens of God's love rather than through the distortion of their wounds. This is the essence of healing. Trauma does not get the final word. People's opinions do not get the final word. The enemy does not get the final word. Only God does.

If you have been categorized by your suffering, it is time to call it what it is—not to minimize it, but to place it in its rightful position under the authority of God's Word. When you say, "It is written," you are declaring that trauma does not own you—God does. Your past does not dictate your future—God does. Your suffering is not your identity—God has already spoken your true identity over you.

Healing begins the moment we take hold of truth and refuse to let go. It is not always an easy battle, but it is a battle we do not fight alone. God has given us His Word, His Spirit, and His promises. The only question is—will we choose to believe what is written?

Reflection Questions for Chapter 6

Personal Reflection

1. Have you ever struggled to name the pain you have experienced? How has avoiding or misidentifying your trauma affected your healing process?

2. In what ways have you allowed past trauma to define your identity? How does recognizing and naming your pain change the way you see yourself?

Spiritual and Biblical Reflection

3. Jesus responded to the enemy's temptations by saying, "It is written." How can you use Scripture to counter the lies trauma has spoken over your life?

4. Psalm 147:3 says, "He heals the brokenhearted and binds up their wounds." How does this truth challenge the way you see your own suffering and the process of healing?

5. How does the example of Jesus resisting temptation in the wilderness (Matthew 4:1-11) demonstrate the power of speaking truth over the pain and struggles in your life?

Healing and Moving Forward

6. What are some practical ways you can replace false narratives about your trauma with the truth of God's Word?

7. Are there specific categories of pain in your life that you have yet to surrender to God? What steps can you take to bring them into the light?

8. How can reframing your suffering through the lens of God's Word help you move from being defined by your past to walking in healing and purpose?

7

REORGANIZED

God has a redeeming power to bring back that which seems unredeemable.

There was a time in my life when I believed that restoration was impossible. The weight of my past, the pain of betrayal, and the wounds I had accumulated along the way all seemed too great for anything good to emerge from them. I had built a life around survival—navigating through pain, managing expectations, and hoping to avoid further hurt. Yet, in my heart, I knew that simply surviving was not what God intended for me. I was stuck, held hostage by past disappointments, unable to move forward because I had not yet allowed God to reorganize my life.

For many who have endured trauma, grief, or loss, the idea of moving forward can feel overwhelming. We cling to what is familiar—even if it is broken—because the unknown can seem too uncertain. But God is not a God of stagnation; He is a God of transformation. He does not simply mend the pieces of our shattered lives; He reorders them, using even the most painful chapters of our stories to bring about something new. This is what it means to be reorganized by God. It is not about erasing the past but about allowing Him to reshape our hearts, our faith, and our future.

God's Power to Restore: How He Reorders What Seems Lost

One of the greatest truths of the gospel is that God specializes in restoration. He takes what is broken and makes it whole again, not by returning it to its original state, but by redeeming it for something greater. The world tells us that some things are too far gone, that certain wounds are irreparable, and that some stories do not deserve redemption. But Scripture tells a different story.

In *Emotionally Healthy Spirituality,* Peter Scazzero (2017) argues that true healing happens not when we simply return to the way things were, but when we allow God to remake us from the inside out. Healing requires deep, internal transformation, not just external change. It is not about covering up wounds but about letting God restructure the very foundation of our lives. This reorganization does not mean returning to who we were before the trauma—it means becoming who we were always meant to be in Christ.

Dallas Willard (1998), in *The Divine Conspiracy,* describes the process of spiritual renewal as one in which God renews the mind and heart, shifting our desires, priorities, and sense of identity. He explains that the work of restoration is not passive; it requires a willingness to partner with God in the process. We must surrender our need for control, release old patterns, and trust that what God is building is better than what was lost.

For those who have walked through trauma, this can feel daunting. The fear of being hurt again can keep us clinging to what is familiar. But Scripture reminds us that

God's power to restore is greater than our fear of change. Isaiah 43:19 (NIV) declares, "See, I am doing a new thing! Now it springs up; do you not perceive it?" God does not simply restore what was—He creates something brand new. When we surrender to His process of reorganization, we begin to see the beauty of His redemptive work.

Mary Magdalene: A Life Reordered by Redemption

One of the most powerful examples of God's ability to reorder a broken life is found in Mary Magdalene. Scripture introduces her as a woman from whom Jesus cast out seven demons (Luke 8:2)—a significant detail that symbolizes complete bondage. Whatever her afflictions had been—whether spiritual oppression, deep emotional wounds, or a painful past—her life had been dominated by darkness. She lived as someone defined by suffering, but when Jesus stepped in, everything changed. He didn't just set her free; He redefined her identity, making her a devoted disciple and a faithful witness of His ministry.

Mary's story reminds us that God does not merely repair what is broken—He reorders it for His divine purpose. She went from a woman bound by demonic possesion to one of Jesus' most faithful followers, remaining by His side even at the cross when many of His disciples had fled (Matthew 27:55-56). But her greatest moment of restoration came after the resurrection. On the morning of Jesus' victory over death, it was Mary who stood weeping outside the empty tomb, overcome with grief (John 20:11-18). Yet, it was in that very place of sorrow that Jesus met her, calling her by name, and commissioning her as the first witness of the resurrection. The risen Savior chose her—once a woman defined by affliction—to become the first to proclaim the greatest news in human history.

Mary's transformation is a testament to God's power to reorder what seems unredeemable. She was not simply healed; she was given a new identity, new purpose, and new mission. Just as Joseph's years of suffering positioned him for a place of influence in Egypt (Genesis 50:20), Mary's personal redemption positioned her for a divine assignment—to carry the message of resurrection and new life to the disciples. Isaiah 61:3 declares that God gives "beauty for ashes" and "turns mourning into joy." In Mary's life, we see this truth displayed—her past did not disqualify her from purpose; rather, it became the backdrop for God's greatest work in her life.

This is the nature of God's restoration. When He reorders a life, He does not simply return it to what it once was. He reshapes it for something greater. Mary Magdalene's transformation is proof that no amount of brokenness, trauma, or past affliction can keep us from the purpose God has for us. Just as Joseph's betrayal led to his promotion, Mary's deliverance led to her divine calling. She reminds us that nothing is beyond redemption, and what the enemy meant for evil, God always turns for good.

Joseph's Rise from Betrayal to Purpose (Genesis 50:20)

Another powerful example of reorganization is found in the life of Joseph. Betrayed by his brothers, sold into slavery, falsely accused, and imprisoned, Joseph endured unimaginable suffering. His pain was not just a singular event—it was a series of injustices that could have easily led him into bitterness, despair, or a cycle of repeating trauma. Yet, through it all, God was working behind the scenes to reorganize Joseph's life for a greater purpose.

By the time Joseph was placed in a position of authority in Egypt, he had been transformed—not just circumstantially, but spiritually. When faced with the brothers who had once betrayed him, he had every reason to seek revenge. Instead, he spoke one of the most profound statements in Scripture: "You intended to harm me, but God intended it for good to accomplish what is now being done, the saving of many lives" (Genesis 50:20, NIV).

Joseph recognized that God had taken what was meant for evil and repurposed it for good. His story is a testimony to the power of divine reorganization—God did not erase Joseph's past, but He used it to position him for something greater.

The same is true for us. Our suffering is not wasted. The wounds we have endured, the betrayals we have faced, and the losses we have grieved are not the end of our stories. God is working behind the scenes, reshaping and repurposing every piece of our pain for something far beyond what we can imagine.

Breaking Cycles of Pain: Moving Beyond Trauma Toward Healing

Trauma has a way of creating cycles. Pain that is not healed often gets passed down—whether through relationships, behaviors, or thought patterns. Many people find themselves stuck, reliving past wounds in new situations, unable to break free from the same struggles. Without intentional healing, what we have suffered can become the framework for how we live, shaping our interactions with God, others, and even ourselves.

In *The Ruthless Elimination of Hurry*, John Mark

Comer (2019) speaks to the necessity of slowing down and creating space for transformation. He explains that one of the reasons many people never move beyond trauma is because they do not take time to process their pain in God's presence. Instead, they fill their lives with busyness, distraction, or unhealthy coping mechanisms, never truly confronting the wounds that need healing. Healing requires intentionality—it is not a passive process but a commitment to breaking cycles of pain and embracing the work of restoration.

Psychologically, breaking cycles requires self-awareness, healing relationships, and a renewed sense of identity. Trauma rewires the brain, affecting how we perceive threats, relationships, and even God. Therapeutic approaches such as Internal Family Systems (IFS) and Cognitive Behavioral Therapy (CBT) emphasize the importance of naming unhealthy patterns and replacing them with life-giving ones. Similarly, spiritual formation requires us to identify the false narratives trauma has written over our lives and replace them with God's truth.

Jesus made this clear when He spoke in John 8:32, "Then you will know the truth, and the truth will set you free." The truth of who we are in Christ must replace the lies trauma has taught us. The lie says, "You will always be broken," but God says, "I make all things new" (Revelation 21:5, NKJV). The lie says, "You are beyond redemption," but God says, "I will restore to you the years that the locusts have eaten" (Joel 2:25, NKJV). The lie says, "Your suffering was wasted," but God says, "I will use it for good" (Genesis 50:20).

When we begin to recognize these patterns and actively speak truth over them, we take the first step toward healing. Trauma no longer holds us captive when we confront it with God's redemptive power.

Takeaway: What the Enemy Meant for Evil, God Can Use for Good.

When we think about reorganization, it is easy to fear change. We may want restoration, but we struggle with the idea of letting go of what is familiar—even if what is familiar is painful. But the truth is this: God is not calling us to return to what was, but to step into what is possible through Him.

The enemy wants us to believe that our suffering defines us. He wants us to remain stuck, convinced that there is no future beyond our trauma. But God is in the business of redemption. He takes what was meant to destroy us and transforms it into the very thing that brings life.

Isaiah 61:3 speaks of giving us "beauty for ashes, the oil of joy for mourning, and the garment of praise for the spirit of despair." This is what it means to be reorganized—to trade in what has been for what God is making new.

If you have ever felt like your life has been reduced to a mess of broken pieces, know this: God is not finished. He is reshaping, restoring, and repurposing every part of your story. What the enemy meant for harm; God will use for good. The only question is—will you allow Him to reorder your life for His glory?

Reflection Questions for Chapter 7

Personal Reflection

1. Think about a time in your life when you felt stuck in survival mode rather than moving toward healing. What kept you from believing that restoration was possible?

2. In what areas of your life do you see the need for God's reorganization? Are there patterns, relationships, or mindsets that He is calling you to release or transform?

Spiritual and Biblical Reflection

3. In Genesis 50:20, Joseph tells his brothers, "You intended to harm me, but God intended it for good." How does this verse challenge your perspective on past suffering? How might God be using your experiences for a greater purpose?

4. Mary Magdalene's life was completely restructured after her encounter with Jesus. How does her story demonstrate the power of redemption? What can you learn from her transformation?

Healing and Moving Forward

5. Breaking cycles of pain requires intentional healing. What practical steps can you take—whether through prayer, counseling,

or spiritual disciplines—to move beyond past trauma toward restoration?

6. John 8:32 says, "Then you will know the truth, and the truth will set you free." What lies from past trauma do you need to replace with God's truth? What scriptures can you use to combat these false beliefs?

7. Dallas Willard describes spiritual renewal as a process of internal transformation. How can you actively participate in the work of healing that God is doing in your life?

8. Isaiah 61:3 speaks of exchanging ashes for beauty. What areas of your life do you need to surrender to God so He can bring beauty from brokenness? How can you begin that process today?

8

STABILIZED

Healing is not about returning to what was, but about stepping into what God has made new.

There was a time in my life when I thought stability meant control—keeping everything in order, managing my emotions, and making sure I didn't experience any more pain than I already had. I equated stability with safety, but what I was really doing was holding onto fear. I didn't want to move forward because I was afraid of falling apart again. The weight of past trauma made me hesitant to embrace anything new, and I spent years trying to hold everything together on my own.

But stability in Christ isn't about self-sufficiency; it's about surrender. True stability is not built on human effort, but on the foundation of God's healing power. We don't find stability by pretending we are unshaken, nor do we find it in avoiding pain. We find it when we learn to trust God, even in the uncertainty of rebuilding our lives.

Many people who have walked through trauma reach a point where they desire healing but fear moving forward. They have spent so much time in survival mode that they struggle to imagine what life could look like beyond their pain. But the journey of healing isn't just about overcoming the past—it's about learning to walk in the new life God has for us. Stability is not a return to what once was; it is a step into what God has made new.

From Chaos to Stability: Learning to Walk in Healing

For many, trauma creates a life that feels chaotic, unpredictable, and exhausting. Emotionally, it can feel like walking on unstable ground, never knowing when the next trigger or setback will come. Spiritually, it can feel like drifting—wanting to trust God but struggling with doubt, fear, and frustration. The instability of trauma can make people hesitant to embrace healing because, in a strange way, suffering can feel familiar.

Peter Scazzero, in *Emotionally Healthy Spirituality* (2017), emphasizes that true healing comes when we allow God to mature us emotionally and spiritually. Many believers focus only on spiritual growth while neglecting emotional healing, leading to a fragile faith that collapses under the weight of unresolved wounds. Stability requires wholeness, and wholeness requires that we address not just our spiritual lives, but our emotional and psychological well-being.

In *Renovation of the Heart,* Dallas Willard (2002) speaks to this process of transformation, reminding us that healing does not happen overnight. God does not simply erase our past; He renews us from the inside out, reshaping our hearts and minds so that we can walk in freedom. Willard emphasizes that true stability is found in surrendering every part of ourselves to God—our emotions, our thoughts, our fears, and our desires.

The key to stability is not perfection, nor is it the absence of hardship. It is found in trusting that God is in control, even when we are not. Psalm 16:8 declares, "I have set the Lord always before me; because he is at my right hand, I shall not be shaken." Stability does not come from avoiding suffering—it comes from keeping our eyes on Christ in the midst of it.

Daniel in the Lion's Den: A Lesson in Stability (Daniel 6)

One of the greatest biblical examples of stability in the face of adversity is found in Daniel's life. Daniel had risen to a place of prominence in the kingdom of Babylon, gaining favor with King Darius. However, his success stirred up jealousy among the other officials, who sought to find a way to bring him down. Knowing that Daniel was faithful to his God, they convinced the king to issue a decree that no one could pray to any god or man except the king for thirty days. The punishment for disobedience? Being thrown into a den of lions.

Daniel had a choice: he could compromise his faith and preserve his life, or he could remain steadfast, trusting that God was greater than the threat before him. Without hesitation, Daniel chose to remain faithful. Scripture tells us that he went home, opened his windows toward Jerusalem, and prayed—just as he had always done (Daniel 6:10). He did not waver. He did not change his behavior out of fear. He remained stable in his faith, despite knowing the consequences.

As expected, Daniel's enemies reported him to the king, and though Darius regretted his decree, he was bound by law to follow through. Daniel was thrown into a den of lions, left to face what should have been certain death. But what happened next revealed the true source of stability—God's sovereign hand.

That night, the king was unable to sleep, deeply distressed over what had happened. At the first light of dawn, he rushed to the den and called out, "Daniel, servant of the living God, has your God, whom you serve continually, been able to rescue you from the lions?" (Daniel 6:20). To his amazement, Daniel responded, "My God sent his angel, and he shut the mouths of the lions" (Daniel 6:22). Not a single scratch was found on Daniel, because, as Scripture says, "he had trusted in his God" (Daniel 6:23, ESV).

Daniel's story is a powerful reminder that stability is not found in our circumstances, but in our confidence in God. The world around him was unstable—his enemies plotted against him, the king's decree threatened his life, and the lion's den represented destruction. Yet, Daniel was unwavering. His faith was not dependent on favorable conditions but on the character of God.

For those who have walked through trauma, fear, or instability, Daniel's story offers a challenge and a promise. The challenge is this: will you remain faithful even when everything around you feels uncertain? Stability is not about avoiding trials but about remaining anchored in the truth of God's sovereignty. The promise is this: when we trust in God, He sustains us. The lions did not disappear, but their power over Daniel was removed. Likewise, our trials may not vanish instantly, but their ability to destroy us is broken when we trust in God's protection.

Just as Daniel walked into the lion's den with unshakable faith, we, too, must walk forward in life with confidence that God is in control. Stability is not the absence of hardship—it is the presence of trust. And when we remain firm in our faith, we will see, just as Daniel did, that God is always faithful to deliver.

Breaking the Cycle of Emotional Instability

For those who have experienced deep trauma, emotional instability can feel like an unavoidable part of life. One day, they may feel strong and capable, only to be overwhelmed by emotions the next. Healing requires learning to break the cycle of instability by developing healthy, godly patterns for processing emotions.

In *The Emotionally Healthy Leader,* Peter Scazzero (2015) highlights that many Christians try to suppress difficult emotions, believing that faith means ignoring pain. However, ignoring emotions does not make them disappear—it only buries them deeper, where they continue to influence thoughts, behaviors, and relationships. Stability requires that we acknowledge our emotions, process them in God's presence, and replace lies with truth.

Similarly, clinical psychology teaches that emotional regulation is a learned skill. Cognitive Behavioral Therapy (CBT) emphasizes identifying unhealthy thought patterns and replacing them with constructive, life-giving ones. When trauma has trained the brain to expect harm, disappointment, or abandonment, individuals must learn to challenge those thoughts with truth. Philippians 4:8 provides a biblical model for this practice: "Whatever is true, whatever is noble, whatever is right, whatever is pure, whatever is lovely, whatever is admirable—if anything is excellent or praiseworthy—think about such things."

Developing emotional stability also requires healthy relationships. Isolation breeds instability, while godly community fosters healing. Proverbs 27:17 (NIV) reminds us, "As iron sharpens iron, so one person sharpens another." Surrounding ourselves with mature, Christ-centered relationships helps anchor us in truth, providing support when old patterns of fear or doubt try to resurface.

Emotional stability is not achieved in isolation; it requires intentional practice and engagement with both biblical truth and psychological principles. In addition to Cognitive Behavioral Therapy (CBT), other therapeutic models such as Dialectical Behavior Therapy (DBT) emphasize mindfulness—training individuals to observe their emotions without being overwhelmed by them. Rather than reacting impulsively to fear, anxiety, or anger, individuals can learn to pause, reflect, and respond in ways that align with their faith and values. The Apostle Paul modeled this practice in 2 Corinthians 10:5, where he instructs believers to "take every thought captive to make it obedient to Christ." When instability creeps in—whether through negative self-talk, triggers from past trauma, or fear of future pain—Christians can cultivate emotional resilience by filtering their thoughts through God's truth.

In addition to renewing the mind, self-awareness is a key component of emotional stability. Peter Scazzero, in *Emotionally Healthy Spirituality* (2017), argues that many Christians struggle with emotional instability because they have not taken time to understand their own inner wounds and triggers. He points out that spiritual maturity and emotional maturity go hand in hand—one cannot thrive without the other. This means that acknowledging emotions, rather than suppressing them, is an essential part of healing. Jesus Himself demonstrated this in Matthew 26:38 (NIV), when He openly expressed His distress before going to the cross: "My soul is overwhelmed with sorrow to the point of death." His willingness to name His emotions, even in the presence of His disciples, shows that true stability is not about pretending to be unaffected by life's struggles but about processing them in God's presence.

Developing emotional stability also requires consistent

spiritual disciplines. Just as physical exercise strengthens the body, spiritual disciplines strengthen the soul, helping individuals remain steady even in the face of hardship. Dallas Willard, in *The Spirit of the Disciplines* (1988), highlights the necessity of practices like prayer, fasting, silence, and solitude as means of cultivating spiritual endurance. These disciplines create space for God to bring peace to chaotic emotions and clarity to distorted thoughts. Jesus modeled this throughout His ministry, frequently withdrawing to pray in moments of stress or pressure (Luke 5:16). When believers make space for God through intentional disciplines, they develop the inner stability necessary to withstand external storms.

Additionally, healthy relationships serve as a stabilizing force in a believer's life. While trauma often isolates, healing happens in community. Dr. Curt Thompson, in *The Soul of Shame* (2015), explains that healing from emotional wounds is best achieved in relationships where individuals are fully known and fully loved. God designed people for connection, and accountability within godly friendships helps break the cycle of negative thinking and emotional instability. Ecclesiastes 4:9-10 (NIV) affirms this truth, stating, "Two are better than one... If either of them falls down, one can help the other up." A strong support system acts as a buffer against the lies of the enemy, reinforcing the truth that no one has to navigate healing alone.

Ultimately, emotional stability is not about the absence of difficulty but about learning to respond to life's challenges with faith and resilience. By engaging in biblical truth, therapeutic wisdom, self-awareness, spiritual disciplines, and Christ-centered community, individuals can move beyond reactive emotional patterns and step into a life of peace, confidence, and unwavering faith in God's promises.

Takeaway: Stability is Found in Trusting God's Plan.

If trauma has made you feel like your life is unstable—if you have spent years walking on shaky ground, fearing the next setback—know this: stability is not found in control, but in trust. It is not about managing every detail of your life so that nothing can go wrong; it is about believing that even if things do go wrong, God is still holding you together.

Psalm 46:1 (NIV) declares, "God is our refuge and strength, an ever-present help in trouble." Stability does not mean the absence of trouble, but the presence of God in every circumstance.

Healing is not just about overcoming trauma; it is about learning to live in the freedom Christ offers. It is about waking up each day and choosing to trust that God is leading you, sustaining you, and working all things together for good. It is about stepping out of the boat and believing that even when the waves rise, you will not sink.

So, where do you go from here? You move forward. Not in fear, but in faith. Not in instability, but in the assurance that God is holding you steady. And no matter what comes, you will not be shaken.

Reflection Questions for Chapter 8

Personal Reflection:

1. In what areas of your life have you sought stability through control rather than trusting in God's provision?

2. How has past trauma influenced the way you respond to uncertainty or emotional instability?

Spiritual and Biblical Reflections:

3. What does Daniel's experience in the lion's den teach you about remaining steadfast in faith during difficult circumstances?

4. How does Psalm 46:1 ("God is our refuge and strength, an ever-present help in trouble") challenge or encourage you in your current season of healing?

Healing and Moving Forward:

5. What practical steps can you take to cultivate emotional stability through spiritual disciplines like prayer, Scripture meditation, or godly community?

6. Who are the "iron sharpens iron" relationships (Proverbs 27:17) in your life that can help anchor you in truth when instability arises?

9

PRIORITIZED

It is time to wake up to important things which make our lives livable again.

There was a time in my life when my priorities were completely misaligned. I was living in survival mode, driven by fear, resentment, and unresolved pain. I wasn't thinking about healing or restoration—I was focused on avoiding further hurt, keeping my defenses up, and proving that I could handle everything on my own. But in the process, I was neglecting the very things that mattered most: my faith, my relationships, and my own well-being.

For many who have walked through trauma, pain becomes the central focus. It dictates emotions, decisions, and even spiritual perspectives. We cling to past wounds, allowing them to shape our identity, often without realizing how much space they occupy in our lives. But there comes a moment when we must decide: Will we continue prioritizing our pain, or will we choose to prioritize healing?

True healing begins when we reevaluate what matters most. It requires an intentional shift—from focusing on the past to embracing the present and the future God has for us. Healing is not just about moving beyond trauma; it's about aligning our lives with God's purpose, placing faith, gratitude, and joy at the center.

Reevaluating Priorities: Placing Faith, Healing, and Purpose Above Past Hurts

One of the most dangerous aspects of trauma is that it convinces us to center our lives around it. Without realizing it, we allow pain to determine our choices, relationships, and even our faith journey. But Scripture calls us to something greater—something beyond just surviving our past.

Jesus addressed this need for prioritization when He said in Matthew 6:33 (NIV), "But seek first his kingdom and his righteousness, and all these things will be given to you as well." This is a radical call to shift our focus from fear to faith, from wounds to worship, and from suffering to surrender.

Peter Scazzero, in *Emotionally Healthy Spirituality* (2017), warns that many believers attempt to live a life of faith while neglecting their inner transformation. They focus on external achievements or religious performance, all while ignoring the deeper work that God wants to do in their hearts. When we prioritize faith, healing, and purpose above our hurts, we begin to see transformation from the inside out.

Reevaluating priorities requires asking hard questions:

- Am I more focused on my past than on God's promises for my future?

- Do I spend more time feeding my pain than feeding my soul?
- Have I allowed bitterness or disappointment to dictate my decisions?
- What would it look like to truly seek God first in every area of my life?

Healing is not just about letting go of the past—it's about intentionally choosing what to hold onto in the present. It's about making room for God to work, allowing Him to shift our focus from what has been lost to what He is restoring.

The Role of Gratitude in Healing: Choosing Joy and Hope

One of the most powerful ways to shift our focus is through gratitude. Gratitude is not about ignoring pain or pretending struggles don't exist—it's about choosing to see God's hand even in the midst of hardship.

Dr. Robert Emmons, a leading researcher on gratitude, found that practicing gratitude rewires the brain, reducing stress and increasing overall well-being. From a biblical perspective, gratitude is a spiritual discipline that keeps our hearts aligned with God. Paul instructs us in 1 Thessalonians 5:16-18 (NIV), "Rejoice always, pray continually, give thanks in all circumstances; for this is God's will for you in Christ Jesus."

Gratitude is not just a response to good things; it is a decision to trust that God is still good even in the midst of suffering. When we practice gratitude, our attitude is transformed, and it allows us to priorize the following as a clear separation from our suffering.

Shift Our Focus from What We Lack to What We Have

One of the greatest struggles for those who have experienced trauma is the tendency to focus on what has been lost. Pain has a way of narrowing our vision, causing us to fixate on the things that didn't go as planned—the relationships that ended, the dreams that fell apart, the stability that was taken away. While it is natural to grieve loss, healing begins when we intentionally shift our focus from what is missing to what remains.

Throughout Scripture, we see this theme echoed. In Lamentations 3:22-23, the prophet Jeremiah writes, "Because of the Lord's great love we are not consumed, for his compassions never fail. They are new every morning; great is your faithfulness." Even in the midst of suffering, Jeremiah chooses to focus not on destruction, but on God's unwavering mercy. This shift in perspective does not erase the pain, but it prevents despair from taking over.

Gratitude plays a crucial role in this transformation. Instead of dwelling on what is absent, we can train our minds to recognize the blessings still present. Maybe the hardship we endured has brought us closer to God. Maybe it has deepened our relationships with those who have stood by us. Maybe it has opened doors to opportunities we never would have considered before. When we begin to focus on the good, we realize that God's provision is still active in our lives.

This shift does not happen passively—it requires practice. Philippians 4:8 (NIV) instructs us, "Whatever is true, whatever is noble, whatever is right, whatever is pure, whatever is lovely, whatever is admirable—if anything is excellent or praiseworthy—think about such things." This is not a call to ignore suffering, but to refuse to let it consume us. As we choose to focus on what we have rather than what we lack, we open the door for healing and hope to take root.

Break the Cycle of Negativity That Trauma Often Creates

Trauma does not just affect the body—it rewires the mind. When a person has been hurt deeply, the brain naturally adapts by anticipating future harm. This often leads to cycles of negative thinking, where one begins to expect disappointment, rejection, or failure at every turn. Over time, these patterns become so ingrained that they shape a person's identity, influencing decisions, relationships, and even their ability to trust God.

Breaking free from these cycles requires intentional effort. Cognitive Behavioral Therapy (CBT) teaches that thought patterns, once identified, can be challenged and replaced with healthier alternatives. The Bible, long before modern psychology, spoke of this same principle. Romans 12:2 urges us, "Do not conform to the pattern of this world, but be transformed by the renewing of your mind." Renewing the mind is a process of replacing old, destructive thoughts with life-giving truth.

One practical way to break the cycle of negativity is through speaking and meditating on Scripture. When the enemy whispers, "You are not enough," we respond with "I am fearfully and wonderfully made" (Psalm 139:14, NKJV). When fear tells us, "You will never heal," we declare, "The Lord is near to the brokenhearted and saves those who are crushed in spirit" (Psalm 34:18). When the past tries to define us, we stand on 2 Corinthians 5:17 (NIV): "If anyone is in Christ, the new creation has come: The old has gone, the new is here!"

In addition to biblical truth, surrounding ourselves with positive influences is essential. Proverbs 13:20 (NIV) states, "Walk with the wise and become wise, for a companion of fools suffers harm." When we engage in uplifting community, worship, and prayer, we disrupt the cycle of negativity. God has not called us to remain stuck in patterns of despair—He has called us into renewal, into transformation, and into the freedom that comes with breaking the chains of destructive thinking.

Strengthen Our Faith by Acknowledging God's Faithfulness

Faith is strengthened in remembrance. Throughout the Bible, God commands His people to remember what He has done. Whether it was the Israelites placing stones of remembrance after crossing the Jordan River (Joshua 4:6-7) or Jesus instituting communion as a way to recall His sacrifice (Luke 22:19), the act of looking back at God's faithfulness fuels trust in His future provision.

When we take time to acknowledge how God has carried us through past difficulties, our faith deepens. We remember the prayers He has answered, the doors He has opened, and the ways He has provided when we saw no way forward. Psalm 77:11-12 (NIV) says, "I will remember the deeds of the Lord; yes, I will remember your miracles of long ago. I will consider all your works and meditate on all your mighty deeds."

One of the biggest challenges in healing is the fear of the unknown. Trauma convinces us that the future will mirror the pain of the past, leading us to hesitate in trusting God's plans. But when we take time to recall how He has sustained us before, we gain confidence that He will do it again. Hebrews 13:8 (NIV) reminds us, "Jesus Christ is the same yesterday and today and forever." If He was faithful then, He will be faithful now.

A practical way to cultivate this mindset is by keeping a record of God's goodness. Journaling answered prayers, unexpected blessings, and moments of peace in chaos helps build a testimony of His faithfulness. This practice not only strengthens personal faith but also provides encouragement to others who may be struggling.

Faith grows when we choose to trust in what God has already done, believing that He will continue His good work in us. As Philippians 1:6 (NIV) assures us, "He who began a good work in you will carry it on to completion until the day of Christ Jesus." When we acknowledge God's faithfulness, we step out of fear and into confidence, knowing that the God who has brought us this far will never abandon us.

By shifting our focus from lack to abundance, breaking the cycle of negativity, and intentionally acknowledging God's faithfulness, we set ourselves on the path toward lasting healing. It is a daily decision to turn from fear to faith, from despair to hope, and from past wounds to God's promises. And as we do, we begin to experience the fullness of the life He has always intended for us.

Dallas Willard, in *The Spirit of the Disciplines* (1988), explains that gratitude is foundational to spiritual transformation. He argues that when we make thanksgiving a daily practice, we open ourselves up to greater joy and healing. Gratitude does not deny the reality of pain, but it refuses to let pain have the final word.

Practicing gratitude may look like:

- Keeping a journal of God's faithfulness, even in small ways.

- Starting each day by thanking God for one thing.
- Speaking words of appreciation to others instead of dwelling on what's wrong.
- Worshiping even when you don't feel like it, declaring God's goodness over your circumstances.

Gratitude is a choice—a daily commitment to acknowledge the goodness of God despite what life has thrown our way. When we make gratitude a priority, healing becomes not just a possibility but a reality.

Mary and Martha—Choosing What Matters Most (Luke 10:38-42)

Perhaps one of the most well-known stories of misplaced priorities in Scripture is the story of Mary and Martha. In Luke 10:38-42, Jesus visits the home of these two sisters. Martha, caught up in the demands of serving, is frustrated that Mary is sitting at Jesus' feet instead of helping with preparations. She complains, asking Jesus to tell Mary to assist her.

But Jesus responds with words that cut to the heart of the matter: "Martha, Martha, you are worried and upset about many things, but few things are needed—or indeed only one. Mary has chosen what is better, and it will not be taken away from her." (Luke 10:41-42, NIV).

Martha's actions weren't wrong—she was doing good work. But she had allowed busyness and distraction to take priority over being present with Jesus. Mary, on the other hand, had chosen what was truly important: sitting at the feet of Christ, receiving from Him.

This story is a reminder that misplaced priorities can rob us of peace, joy, and healing. Many people who have experienced trauma function like Martha—constantly striving, staying busy, and focusing on external things while neglecting the deeper work God wants to do in them. They may fill their lives with distractions, avoiding the pain that still lingers.

But healing requires a Mary posture—one that prioritizes being in God's presence over simply doing things for Him. It means slowing down, resting in His grace, and allowing Him to restore what has been broken.

Takeaway: Aligning Our Lives with God's Purpose Brings Healing.

At some point in the healing journey, a choice must be made: Will we continue to let our pain define us, or will we choose to prioritize the things that bring life?

The enemy wants us stuck—distracted, overwhelmed, and focused on everything except what truly matters. But God calls us into something greater. He calls us to:

- *Prioritize faith over fear*. Trusting that God's plan is greater than our past.
- *Prioritize healing over avoidance*. Facing pain with the confidence that God is restoring us.
- *Prioritize gratitude over bitterness*. Choosing to see the goodness of God even in difficult seasons.
- *Prioritize purpose over passivity*. Walking in the calling He has placed on our lives.

When we realign our lives with God's purpose, we begin to experience healing in ways we never imagined.

Psalm 90:12 (NKJV) says, "Teach us to number our days, that we may gain a heart of wisdom." This verse reminds us that our time is valuable, and we must choose wisely how we spend it.

If trauma has consumed your thoughts, if pain has dictated your priorities, today is the day to realign. It's time to wake up to the things that make life livable again—faith, gratitude, purpose, and hope. It's time to let go of what has been and embrace what God is doing now.

Because when we choose what is most important, when we sit at the feet of Jesus like Mary, we discover that healing isn't just about recovering from the past—it's about stepping fully into the life God has always intended for us.

Reflection Questions for Chapter 9

Personal Reflection

1. What past hurts or experiences have you been unintentionally prioritizing over your faith, healing, and purpose? How has this affected your spiritual and emotional well-being?

2. In what ways has trauma influenced your daily decisions, relationships, and mindset? Are there areas where you need to shift your focus toward healing and growth?

Spiritual and Biblical Reflection

3. Reflect on the story of Mary and Martha (Luke 10:38-42). Are you more like Martha—constantly busy and distracted—or like Mary, prioritizing time with Jesus? How can you create more space to sit at His feet?

4. How does gratitude play a role in your healing journey? Consider 1 Thessalonians 5:16-18. What are three things you can thank God for today, even in the midst of challenges?

Healing and Moving Forward

5. What practical steps can you take to break the cycle of negativity and refocus your

mind on God's truth?

6. How can you apply Philippians 4:8 in your daily thought patterns?

7. What specific areas of your life need realignment with God's purpose? How can you begin prioritizing faith, healing, and gratitude over fear, pain, and past struggles?

10

MOBILIZED

God's Spirit is upon us to mobilize our heart, body, and soul to accomplish what He has called us to do.

I remember the moment when I realized healing wasn't just about me. It wasn't just about overcoming my own struggles or making peace with my past. It was about something bigger—something beyond myself.

For a long time, I thought healing meant reaching a place where I no longer felt the pain, where I had fully processed my wounds and could finally move on. But as God was restoring me, He began to stir something new within me—an urgency, a calling, a sense that there was more. I had spent so much time focusing on getting better, but I hadn't yet asked what I was supposed to do with my healing.

Then, one day, it hit me: healing isn't the destination—it's the launching point.

God doesn't restore us just so we can be whole for ourselves; He heals us so we can step into the purpose He has for us. He binds up our wounds so we can walk forward in faith, ready to serve, ready to help, and ready to pour out what we've received. I realized that my pain had not been wasted. Every struggle, every battle, every moment of suffering had been shaping me for something greater.

That was the turning point. That was when I knew: it was time to stop just thinking about healing and start living it out. It was time to mobilize.

And maybe that's where you are right now—standing on the edge of healing, wondering what comes next. The answer? It's time to move.

Now is the time to step into the calling God has placed on your life. Now is the time to take all that He has done in you and allow Him to use it through you. Because healing is not where the journey ends—it is where purpose begins.

From Healing to Action: Taking Steps Toward Purpose

Healing is not the end of the journey—it is the beginning of something greater. For too long, pain may have kept us stuck, immobilized by fear, insecurity, or doubt. But God never intended for healing to be where we stop; He calls us to move forward, to step into the purpose that He has been preparing us for all along.

For those who have experienced trauma, taking action can feel intimidating. After spending so much time in survival mode, the idea of stepping into something new—something uncertain—can bring anxiety. Yet, Scripture is clear that God does not restore us just for our own sake; He restores us so that we can be His hands and feet in the world. Isaiah 61:1 (NIV) declares, "The Spirit of the Sovereign Lord is on me, because the Lord has anointed me to proclaim good news to the poor. He has sent me to bind up the brokenhearted, to proclaim freedom for the captives and release from darkness for the prisoners."

God does not heal us just so we can return to comfort—He heals us so that we can be part of His redemptive work in the lives of others. Healing is a doorway to purpose. But in order to step through it, we must choose to move forward.

One of the most common lies that trauma tells us is that we are not ready—that we need more time, more healing, more preparation before we can do what God has called us to do. While wisdom calls for seasons of rest and renewal, it also reminds us that there comes a time when we must step out in faith. Healing is not about waiting for the perfect moment; it is about trusting that God is already working through us as we move.

The key to mobilization is recognizing that God does not call us once we are fully healed—He calls us in the midst of our healing. When we step forward in faith, we do not do so in our own strength, but in His. The wounds that once immobilized us become testimonies that empower others. The areas of pain that once defined us become markers of His redemption. As we take steps of obedience, we experience the fulfillment of our healing—not just as a personal victory, but as part of God's greater story.

Faith in Motion: The Importance of Walking in Obedience

Faith is not static—it requires movement. Throughout Scripture, God's people were called not just to believe, but to act on that belief. Abraham had to leave his homeland before he saw the fulfillment of God's promise (Genesis 12:1-4). Peter had to step out of the boat before he could walk on water (Matthew 14:29). The ten lepers had to walk in obedience before they received their healing (Luke 17:14). In every case, faith required action.

James 2:17 (NIV) reminds us, "Faith by itself, if it is not accompanied by action, is dead." Healing cannot be fully realized if we remain stagnant. When God restores us, He calls us to put that restoration into motion—whether through serving, leading, encouraging, or stepping into the purpose He has designed for us.

However, moving forward does not mean rushing ahead without direction. Dallas Willard, in *Hearing God: Developing a Conversational Relationship with God* (1999), explains that walking in obedience requires a deep, intimate connection with God. He emphasizes that spiritual formation is not about hurried activity, but about listening, discerning, and responding to God's leading. Mobilization does not mean moving for the sake of movement—it means aligning our steps with God's purpose.

When we walk in obedience, we step into a rhythm of faith that propels us forward. We begin to see opportunities that we once missed. We recognize divine appointments where God is calling us to minister, to encourage, and to lead. Healing is not just about overcoming the past—it is about stepping into what God is doing now.

Nehemiah: Rebuilding the Walls of Jerusalem (Nehemiah 2-6)

One of the most powerful biblical examples of mobilization is found in the story of Nehemiah. When Nehemiah learned that the walls of Jerusalem were in ruins, he was deeply burdened. Though he was serving in a position of influence as the cupbearer to the king of Persia, he knew that God was calling him to take action.

Rather than sitting in despair or waiting for someone else to fix the problem, Nehemiah prayed and then moved. He sought the king's permission to return to Jerusalem, gathered resources, and began the work of rebuilding. His heart had been broken for his people, but instead of remaining in sorrow, he allowed God to mobilize him into action.

Rebuilding the walls was not an easy task. Nehemiah faced opposition from enemies who mocked and threatened him. There were moments when the people were discouraged, weary from the labor. But Nehemiah remained steadfast, urging them to continue the work. He declared in Nehemiah 2:18 (NIV), "I also told them about the gracious hand of my God on me and what the king had said to me. They replied, 'Let us start rebuilding.' So, they began this good work."

Nehemiah's story teaches us that stepping into action does not mean the absence of difficulty. We will face challenges, resistance, and moments of doubt. But like Nehemiah, we must be willing to do the work. He did not wait for the walls to be rebuilt on their own—he mobilized the people, strategized against opposition, and kept moving forward in faith.

For those who have walked through seasons of pain, Nehemiah's story is a reminder that God calls us to rise from the ashes and build. He does not leave us in ruins. Instead, He equips us to restore what has been broken—not just in our own lives, but in the lives of others. Healing is not just about personal renewal; it is about becoming part of God's mission to bring restoration to the world around us.

Takeaway: God Heals So We Can Help Others.

Healing is never just for us. Throughout Scripture, those who encountered God's transformative power were called to share that experience with others. The Samaritan woman at the well (John 4) was not just healed from her past—she became a messenger of Christ's love to her community. Paul was not just redeemed from his mistakes—he was mobilized to spread the gospel across the known world. Peter was not just restored after denying Jesus—he was commissioned to lead the early church.

When God restores, He sends.

When He heals, He equips.

When He transforms, He mobilizes.

If you have experienced healing, it is not just for your own comfort—it is because there is someone else who needs to hear your story, see your faith, and be encouraged by your journey. 2 Corinthians 1:4 reminds us, "He comforts us in all our troubles so that we can comfort those in any trouble with the comfort we ourselves receive from God."

Healing is not passive; it is active. It calls us to move, to give, to serve, and to step into the work that God has prepared for us.

So where do you go from here?

You take the next step.

It does not have to be a grand, overwhelming leap. It can be as simple as saying yes to an opportunity, reaching out to someone who needs encouragement, or stepping into a new area of service. It can be starting a conversation, joining a ministry, or using your gifts in ways you never thought possible.

The key is movement.

God did not heal you to remain where you were. He healed you to step into the fullness of what He has for you. The question now is: Will you go?

Because the world is waiting.

And you are ready.

Reflection Questions for Chapter 10

Personal Reflection

1. Looking back on your healing journey, what has God restored in you that you once thought was lost?

2. In what areas of your life have you felt a stirring to move forward, but fear or hesitation has held you back?

Spiritual and Biblical Reflections

3. Nehemiah saw the broken walls of Jerusalem and felt called to rebuild them. What "broken walls" in your life or community is God calling you to restore?

4. How does James 2:17 ("Faith by itself, if it is not accompanied by action, is dead") challenge your understanding of faith and obedience in your healing journey?

Healing and Moving Forward

5. Healing is not just about personal renewal—it is about stepping into God's purpose. How can you use your healing to serve or encourage others?

6. What is one practical step you can take this week to walk in obedience to God's calling on your life?

7. Reflect on 2 Corinthians 1:4: "He comforts us in all our troubles so that we can comfort those in any trouble with the comfort we ourselves receive from God." How might your past pain be preparing you to help someone else?

8. What fears or doubts do you need to surrender to God in order to fully step into the purpose He has for you?

11

DEPUTIZED

We are not only healed, we are commissioned to carry His authority, His compassion, and His power into a broken world.

There was a time when I doubted whether God could ever use someone like me. I had been through too much—too much failure, too much pain, too much regret. I figured I was better off in the background, quietly trying to rebuild what had been broken. But one day, in prayer, I sensed the Lord speaking directly to my heart: "I've not only healed you—I've called you." That moment changed everything. I began to realize that God wasn't waiting for me to be perfect; He was simply asking me to say yes. He was inviting me to represent Him—to carry His love, His power, and His name into places that desperately needed hope. I was no longer just a survivor—I was His ambassador. That shift from healed to deputized was a turning point. It wasn't about earning a position; it was about stepping into an identity that had always been mine in Christ.

All authority in heaven and on earth has been given to Me. Therefore go…

— Matthew 28:18–19 (ESV)

When God begins to heal and mobilize us, it is not merely so we can walk in wholeness for our own benefit—it is so that we can walk in authority for the sake of others. After we've been restored, we are not sent out empty-handed. We are deputized—commissioned and empowered by Jesus Christ to represent His name, His authority, and His Kingdom here on earth.

To be deputized means to be given official authority to act on behalf of someone else. In the kingdom of God, that Someone is Jesus. As His ambassadors, we don't go in our own strength or wisdom. We go in His name. Jesus made it clear in Matthew 28:18–20 that "all authority in heaven and on earth" had been given to Him—and then He transferred that authority to us as His disciples: "Go therefore…" We are not only saved, not only sent—we are also empowered.

Being deputized by Christ means we are clothed in spiritual authority that isn't dependent on our title, past, or perfection. It is rooted in our relationship with Jesus and the power of the Holy Spirit. In Luke 10:19, Jesus said, "I have given you authority to trample on snakes and scorpions and to overcome all the power of the enemy." He wasn't just talking to the twelve apostles—He was speaking to all those He sends out in His name. That includes you.

Empowered by the Spirit, Commissioned by the Son

Acts 1:8 reminds us, "You will receive power when the Holy Spirit comes on you; and you will be my witnesses." The word for "power" here is Dunamis, from which we get the word "dynamite." This is not mere symbolic empowerment—it is explosive, life-transforming power. When we receive the Holy Spirit, we don't just receive comfort or conviction—we receive the capacity to act on Jesus' behalf with courage, compassion, and clarity.

As those who have been healed and mobilized, we now carry the authority to walk into dark places with light, to speak peace into chaos, and to bring hope into hopeless situations. We are deputized not just to survive our own pain but to invade the enemy's territory and take back what was stolen—not just for us, but for others too.

This is why your story matters. This is why your healing has purpose. You are not simply a recipient of grace—you are now a carrier of it.

The King's Signet Ring

Imagine a servant in a kingdom who has endured great hardship and rejection. One day, the king calls this servant into his throne room—not to reprimand him, but to commission him. The king takes off his signet ring and places it on the servant's finger. With that ring comes the king's authority. Now, when the servant speaks, he speaks on behalf of the king. When he delivers messages or carries out tasks, others recognize the authority of the throne backing him.

You are that servant. Jesus, the King of Kings, has called you into His presence—not just to heal your wounds, but to commission you for purpose. He places His authority upon your life—not in the form of a physical ring, but in the form of His Spirit and His name. You now carry the message of the King, empowered to speak life, declare healing, and bring others out of darkness into light.

This is not a symbolic appointment. It is spiritual reality. You are deputized.

Jesus Wants You to Represent His Love

Perhaps one of the most humbling truths of the gospel is that Jesus chooses to partner with us in His redemptive mission. He could have healed the world in an instant. He could have sent angels to proclaim His name. But instead, He deputized broken, healed, and willing vessels like us to carry out His purpose on earth.

Why? Because He wants people to see what grace looks like with skin on. He wants them to see love in action, hope in motion, and redemption lived out. Through your life, others will come to know that Jesus sees them, loves them, and desires to bring them out of the ashes and into the beauty of His holiness.

This is not a burden—it is a privilege. Jesus trusts you with His message. He trusts you with His mission. And because of that, you can walk in confidence, knowing that the same authority that raised Christ from the dead now empowers you to live, lead, and love in His name.

Takeaway: You Have Been Deputized to Walk in Christ's Authority

When God heals you, He doesn't stop there—He calls

you, equips you, and sends you. You are not just a survivor of your pain; you are an ambassador of Jesus Christ, carrying His authority, His love, and His message of redemption into the world. Just as a deputy carries the seal of the one who sent them, you have been deputized by the King of Kings to speak life, bring hope, and walk in power.

You don't go in your own strength. You go in His name.

The authority of Jesus is not reserved for the few—it is available to all who believe. Through the empowerment of the Holy Spirit, you are not only made whole, but you are made ready. Ready to declare freedom to the captives. Ready to carry beauty into brokenness. Ready to speak resurrection over dead places.

You are no longer standing in the ashes—you are rising with purpose, clothed in authority, and filled with His Spirit.

You have been deputized. Now go walk in it.

Reflection Questions for Chapter 11

Personal Reflection

1. Have you ever sensed that God wanted to use you in ways that felt intimidating or beyond your comfort zone? What held you back?

2. In what ways has your personal healing journey uniquely equipped you to represent Christ to others?

Spiritual and Biblical Reflection

3. Read Matthew 28:18–20 and Luke 10:19. What do these passages reveal about the authority believers carry through Jesus?

4. Reflect on the image of the King's signet ring. How does this illustration challenge or affirm your understanding of your spiritual identity?

Healing and Moving Forward

5. What might change in your life if you fully believed that you are deputized by Christ to carry His name and power?

6. Who in your life may need to experience the love and authority of Jesus through your story or ministry?

12

UTILIZED

A purposeful God calls us to have a purpose even after tragedy.

There was a time when I wondered if my story had any value beyond my own personal struggle. I had walked through pain, experienced loss, and carried wounds that I thought had disqualified me from making a difference. I believed that my suffering had taken something from me—my confidence, my voice, my sense of purpose. But over time, God began to reveal something I never expected: my pain was not the end of my story; it was the foundation of my calling.

At first, I resisted the idea. I didn't want my wounds to define me, and I certainly didn't want them to be the thing that propelled me forward. But God had other plans. I started to notice how the very things I had suffered became the points of connection with others. My story—once a source of shame—became a bridge for healing. The lessons I had learned in the dark became light for someone else's path. The prayers I had whispered in desperation became the words of encouragement I could now offer to others.

It was then that I understood a crucial truth: God never

wastes a wound. Every experience, every battle, every scar carries the potential to be used for His glory. He does not allow suffering without purpose; instead, He redeems it, transforming pain into ministry and brokenness into testimony.

And so, I made a decision. I would not let my past hold me back. I would not let my pain be wasted. If God could use me—even in my weakness—then I would say yes. And in that moment of surrender, I stepped into something far greater than I could have imagined: the realization that my life was meant to be utilized for His purpose.

Turning Pain into Ministry: Using Our Testimony to Encourage Others

There is power in a redeemed story. Many of us assume that our struggles disqualify us from making a difference, but in reality, our struggles prepare us to minister to others in a way that nothing else can. The greatest ministries are often born from the deepest wounds.

Paul reminds us of this truth in 2 Corinthians 1:3-4 (NIV), where he writes:

"Praise be to the God and Father of our Lord Jesus Christ, the Father of compassion and the God of all comfort, who comforts us in all our troubles, so that we can comfort those in any trouble with the comfort we ourselves receive from God."

Pain can make us bitter, or it can make us ministers. It can cause us to withdraw, or it can push us forward into our purpose. The difference lies in whether we allow God to redeem our suffering. When we surrender our wounds to Him, He transforms them into tools for healing.

Think about the people who have impacted your faith journey. Chances are, many of them have experienced suffering. Their testimonies, their wisdom, and their ability to walk with others through difficult seasons often come from their own battles. The best encouragers are those who have been encouraged, the best comforters are those who have been comforted, and the best ministers are those who have been ministered to.

When we are willing to share our story, we give others permission to hope. We remind them that they are not alone. We become living proof that God restores, that healing is possible, and that there is life beyond the pain. Our testimony is not just about what we've been through—it's about what God has done through it.

The Call to Serve: Finding Meaning in Helping Those Who Struggle

One of the most powerful ways to heal is to help others heal. Service is not just an act of kindness; it is an act of restoration. When we step out of our own pain to lift someone else up, we participate in God's redemptive work.

In Matthew 20:28 (NIV), Jesus said, "The Son of Man did not come to be served, but to serve, and to give his life as a ransom for many." If Jesus, who was fully God, chose a life of service, then how much more are we called to do the same?

Serving does not mean ignoring our pain or pretending it never happened. Instead, it means allowing our pain to become a catalyst for compassion. It means choosing to be present for those who are struggling, offering the same grace and encouragement that we once needed.

Many people hesitate to step into service because they feel unqualified. They assume that they need more healing, more training, or more experience before they can help others. But the truth is, God doesn't call the qualified—He qualifies the called. If He has placed a burden on your heart to serve, then He will equip you to do it.

Service can take many forms. It can be as simple as listening to someone who is hurting, mentoring someone walking through a similar struggle, or using your talents to uplift others. It can be leading a support group, volunteering in your community, or even sharing your story through writing, speaking, or discipleship. Whatever it looks like, one thing is certain: when we step into serving, we step into healing.

Serving shifts our focus from what we have lost to what we can give. It takes the attention off of our pain and places it on others who need hope. And in the process, we find that the very thing we thought disqualified us is what God uses to equip us.

Paul's Transformation from Persecutor to Preacher (Acts 9)

Perhaps one of the most profound examples of a life utilized for God's purpose is found in the story of Paul. Before his encounter with Christ, Paul—then called Saul—was a persecutor of Christians. He was known for his zeal in opposing the gospel, hunting down believers, and approving their executions. If there was ever someone who seemed beyond redemption, it was Saul.

But then, everything changed.

In Acts 9 (NIV), Saul was traveling to Damascus when he was suddenly blinded by a great light. He fell to the ground and heard the voice of Jesus saying, "Saul, Saul, why do you persecute me?" This encounter left Saul completely transformed. He was led to Damascus, where God sent Ananias to restore his sight and commission him into ministry.

The man who once sought to destroy the church became one of its greatest builders. The persecutor became a preacher. The enemy of Christ became His most devoted apostle. And the very thing that had once defined Saul's life—his zealous opposition to Christianity—became the testimony that fueled his ministry.

Paul's story teaches us that no one is beyond redemption. It shows us that God can take even the most broken past and use it for His glory. Paul did not let his former mistakes keep him from stepping into his calling. Instead, he allowed God to redefine his life.

Just as Paul was once blinded before he could truly see, we too must experience transformation before we can fully step into our purpose. The pain we have walked through, the lessons we have learned, and the healing we have received all prepare us for the work ahead. God does not waste our suffering. He redeems it and mobilizes us for His mission.

Takeaway: God Never Wastes a Wound—He Redeems It for His Glory.

If you have ever felt like your pain was pointless, if you have ever wondered whether your story has value, let this truth settle into your heart: God never wastes a wound.

Every struggle, every loss, every moment of suffering carries the potential for redemption. What the enemy meant for evil, God will use for good (Genesis 50:20). Your story is not over. In fact, it is just beginning.

The question is—will you let God use it?

Will you allow your pain to become a testimony? Will you step into serving others, even if you don't feel fully ready? Will you trust that God is calling you to something greater, even after all you have been through?

Because here's the truth: You are not here by accident. The experiences you have endured, the battles you have fought, and the healing you have received are all part of a bigger plan. God is writing a redemption story in your life. And now, He is calling you to step into it.

So go. Share your story. Serve with love. Walk in purpose because a purposeful God has given you a purpose—even after tragedy.

Reflection Questions for Chapter 12

Personal Reflection

1. How has your pain shaped your perspective on life, faith, and purpose? Are there areas where you still struggle to see God's redemptive hand at work?

2. In what ways have you seen God use past challenges to equip you for something greater? How has your healing journey prepared you to encourage others?

Spiritual and Biblical Reflection

3. Consider Paul's transformation in Acts 9. How does his story of redemption and purpose encourage you in your own faith journey?

4. Reflect on 2 Corinthians 1:3-4—how does this passage challenge or inspire you to use your story to comfort others?

5. What biblical examples of redemption and purpose resonate most with you? How do they shape your understanding of how God uses brokenness for His glory?

Healing and Moving Forward

6. What steps can you take to turn your past pain into a ministry that blesses others?

7. Have you been hesitant to serve because you feel unqualified or "not ready"? How does God's ability to use imperfect people encourage you to step forward?

8. In what ways can you begin serving now, even in small ways, to allow God to use your story for His purpose?

EPILOGUE: *Resurrection of Dead Dreams*

What seems to be the end of our world can actually become the beginning of the Holy Spirit's resurrection of our dead dreams.

I never thought I would stand on the other side of my pain and see anything worth redeeming. There were seasons in my life when the dreams I once held so tightly seemed buried beneath disappointment, rejection, and loss. I had prayed, planned, and pursued what I believed was my calling, only to watch pieces of it crumble before me. I grieved not just the circumstances but the version of myself that had once believed anything was possible.

When you've experienced deep hurt, it's easy to assume that your best days are behind you. The passion that once fueled you fades into exhaustion. The faith that once felt unshakable is tested by unanswered prayers. And the dreams you once dared to chase seem foolish in light of the reality of setbacks. I reached a point where I stopped believing that God had more for me. I wasn't angry with Him—I was just weary. I was tired of hoping. Tired of trying. Tired of waiting for something that felt like it would never come.

But God was not done.

What I saw as the end, He saw as preparation. What I labeled as a failure, He redefined as transformation. I thought my dreams had been buried for good, but what I didn't realize was that they were merely being planted—waiting for the right season to bloom. It took time for me to see it, but when I did, I realized that nothing I had walked through had been wasted. The heartbreak, the disappointments, the moments I thought I had lost it all—God had been using every single one to shape me for what was ahead.

And maybe that's where you are today. Maybe you've been standing among the ruins of what you once hoped for, believing that it's too late for things to change. Maybe you've settled into the idea that certain dreams will never be resurrected. But I'm here to tell you: God is not finished with you.

The dreams He placed in your heart were not accidents. The purpose He created you for has not expired. And the story He is writing with your life is still unfolding. What you thought was dead—what you thought was over—can still be revived.

Because we serve a God of resurrection.

God's Power to Revive: Dreams, Callings, and Hope That Seemed Lost

There are moments in life when everything feels like it has come to an end. The dreams we once held onto slip through our fingers, our calling seems distant, and hope feels like an illusion. We stand among the wreckage of what we thought life would be, wondering if anything can ever be rebuilt. The weight of loss—whether it be the loss of purpose, vision, or even faith—can make it seem as though the best days are behind us. But the story of redemption tells a different truth: with God, nothing is beyond resurrection.

The very nature of God is to restore, to breathe new life into what we thought was finished. Throughout Scripture, we see His power at work—taking what was broken, what was barren, what was lifeless, and making it new. He does not just mend; He resurrects. What we see as the end, He sees as a new beginning.

One of the biggest lies the enemy tells us is that because we have faced failure, heartbreak, or devastation, our story is over. But God specializes in making impossible situations the very soil where new things grow. In Isaiah 43:19 (NIV), He declares, "See, I am doing a new thing! Now it springs up; do you not perceive it?" Even when we cannot see the evidence of resurrection yet, God is already at work, preparing something beyond what we could have imagined.

If you have ever believed that your best days are behind you, that your calling has expired, or that your dreams have been buried too deep to be revived, let this be a reminder: the same God who rolled away the stone from the tomb still moves stones today. What looks like the end may very well be the beginning of something far greater.

Looking Back at How God Worked Through the Hardest Moments

Looking back on my own journey, I remember times when I was convinced that certain dreams were dead. I had poured myself into things that didn't work out, invested in people who walked away, and believed for things that never came to pass. There were seasons when I questioned whether I had misunderstood my calling altogether—if maybe I had misheard God or if my failures had disqualified me from His plans.

But with time, I began to see something unexpected. The places where I thought I had lost the most were the very places where God was preparing me for something greater. What felt like dead ends were actually detours leading me exactly where I needed to be. The things I grieved—whether opportunities, relationships, or plans—were not wasted. They were transformed.

I didn't see it then, but now I know: God was not rejecting my dreams. He was refining them. He was taking the things I had clung to and replacing them with something better. He was allowing certain doors to close, not to leave me empty, but to prepare me for doors I hadn't even considered.

Every broken piece, every disappointment, and every season of waiting had purpose. They shaped me. They deepened my faith. And they made room for something new.

If you are in a season where you feel like your dreams have been buried, I want to encourage you: wait. Watch. Trust. You may not see it now, but resurrection is coming. God is still writing your story. What seems lost today may very well be preparing you for something greater tomorrow.

Ezekiel's Vision of Dry Bones (Ezekiel 37:1-14, NIV)

Few passages in Scripture capture the essence of resurrection quite like Ezekiel's vision of the valley of dry bones. The prophet Ezekiel is taken by the Spirit of the Lord to a valley filled with lifeless, scattered bones—remnants of what once was. It is a picture of utter devastation, a symbol of lost hope.

Then, God asks a powerful question: "Son of man, can these bones live?" (Ezekiel 37:3).

Ezekiel, looking at the impossibility of the situation, responds, "Sovereign Lord, you alone know."

What happens next is nothing short of miraculous. God commands Ezekiel to prophesy over the bones, and as he speaks, the bones begin to come together. Tendons form, flesh appears, and bodies take shape—but they are still lifeless. Then, God tells Ezekiel to prophesy again, this time calling for the breath of life. As he obeys, breath enters the bodies, and they stand on their feet—a vast army, fully alive.

God explains that these bones represent the people of Israel, who had lost all hope, saying, "Our bones are dried up and our hope is gone; we are cut off" (Ezekiel 37:11). But God declares His promise: "I will put my Spirit in you and you will live, and I will settle you in your own land" (Ezekiel 37:14).

This passage is not just about Israel—it is about us. How often do we look at our circumstances and believe that restoration is impossible? How often do we stand in the middle of what looks like lifeless remains, convinced that hope is gone? But just as God breathed life into dry bones, He breathes life into our weary souls.

No dream is too far gone. No calling is too broken. No situation is beyond His reach. What He did for those bones, He can do for us.

But notice this: the bones did not come to life until Ezekiel obeyed and spoke the word of the Lord over them. There is power in what we declare over our own lives. We must choose to speak life over what appears lifeless.

We must choose to believe that resurrection is possible. And when we do, we will see God move in ways we never expected.

Trust That Beauty Will Rise from the Ashes

This is not the end of your story. The disappointments, the delays, the detours—none of it is wasted. God is a master of resurrection, and what seems dead today is often the very thing He will use to display His glory tomorrow.

Isaiah 61:3 (NKJV) declares that He gives "beauty for ashes, the oil of joy for mourning, and the garment of praise for the spirit of despair." This is the heart of God—to take what has been broken and make it beautiful again.

Maybe you feel like you've lost too much. Maybe you've convinced yourself that your best days are behind you. Maybe you've grown weary of hoping, tired of waiting, and hesitant to believe that restoration is possible. But let me remind you: your story is not over.

What seemed to have died in one season can be resurrected in another. What was buried in grief can rise again in purpose. What looked like an ending can become a new beginning.

Trust that the God who breathes life into dry bones is breathing life into you. Trust that the dreams He placed in your heart are not forgotten.Trust that beauty will rise from the ashes. And trust that the best is still to come.

REFERENCES

Allender, D. B. (1999). The healing path: How the hurts in your past can lead you to a more abundant life WaterBrook Press.

Brown, B. (2012). Daring greatly: How the courage to be vulnerable transforms the way we live, love, par ent, and lead. Gotham Books.

Cloud, H. (1992). Changes that heal: Four practical steps to a healthier you. Zondervan.

Cloud, H., & Townsend, J. (1995). Safe people: How to find relationships that are good for you and avoid those that aren't.

Cloud, H., & Townsend, J. (1992). Boundaries: When to say yes, how to say no to take control of your life. Zondervan.

Comer, J. M. (2024). The practicing way: Be with Jesus, become like him, do as he did. WaterBrook.

Comer, J. M. (2019). The ruthless elimination of hurry: How to stay emotionally healthy and spiritually alive in the chaos of the modern world. WaterBrook.

Crabb, L. J. (1997). Connecting: Healing for ourselves and our relationships. Word Publishing. Foster, R. J. (2018). Celebration of discipline: The path to spir itual growth. HarperOne.

Crabb, L. (2001). Shattered dreams: God's unexpected path to joy. WaterBrook Press.

Crossway Bibles. (2001). The Holy Bible, English Standard Version. Crossway.

Dobbins, J. (2024). Hope after church hurt: How to heal, reengage, and rediscover God's heart for you. Baker Books.

Emmons, R. A. (2007). Thanks!: How the new science of gratitude can make you happier. Houghton Mifflin Harcourt.

Fleece Allen, E. (2017). No more faking fine: Ending the pretending. Zondervan.

Keller, T. (2013). Walking with God through pain and suffering. Dutton

McMahan, O. (1995). Scriptural counseling: A God-centered method. Pathway Press.

McMahan, O., & Hughes, J. C. (1996). The caring

Christian: A guide to helping and healing. Pathway Press.

McMahan, O. (1999). A caring church: Helping churches become healing communities. Pathway Press.

McMahan, O. (2005). Becoming a shepherd: Leadership lessons from the Good Shepherd. Pathway Press.

New International Version. (2011). The Holy Bible, New International Version. Biblica, Inc.

New King James Version. (1982). The Holy Bible, New King James Version. Thomas Nelson.

Scazzero, P. (2015). The emotionally healthy leader: How transforming your inner life will deeply transform your church, team, and the world. Zondervan.

Scazzero, P. (2017). Emotionally healthy spirituality: It's impossible to be spiritually mature while remaining emotionally immature. Zondervan.

Taylor, M. A. (2023). A summary of ministers with trauma and their journey to trauma recovery and greater success in their ministry context. Pentecostal Theo logical Seminary.

TerKeurst, L. (2018). It's not supposed to be this way: Finding unexpected strength when disappointments leave you shattered. Thomas Nelson.

Thompson, C. (2015). The soul of shame: Retelling the stories we believe about ourselves. IVP Books.

Townsend, J. (2019). People fuel: Fill your tank for life, love, and leadership. Zondervan.

Willard, D. (1998). The divine conspiracy: Rediscovering our hidden life in God. HarperOne

Willard, D. (2002). Renovation of the heart: Putting on the character of Christ. NavPress.

Willard, D. (1988). The spirit of the disciplines: Under standing how God changes lives. HarperOne.

Wilson, J. A. (2021). Evading trouble. Kingdom Publishin

About the Author

Dr. Mark A. Taylor is a pastor, clinician, and speaker who has dedicated his life to ministering to the broken and walking alongside those who have experienced deep trauma. His calling is rooted in Isaiah 61:1-3 and Luke 4:18-19 (KJV), where Jesus declares His mission to set at liberty those who are bruised. These verses have shaped not only his ministry but his personal journey of redemption, restoration, and purpose.

As an ordained bishop with the Church of God (Cleveland, TN) and the Lead Pastor of Thrive Church of God in Visalia, California, Mark has served in pastoral leadership for over two decades, preaching the gospel with a heart for those who feel abandoned, wounded, or disqualified by life's struggles. His ministry emphasizes the intersection of faith, mental health, and trauma-informed care, providing a safe space for people to encounter God's healing presence. He also currently serves the CA/NV Church of God Region as Ministerial Care Director.

In addition to his pastoral work, Mark is a Licensed Professional Clinical Counselor (LPCC) as an experienced therapist, crisis mental health practitioner, specializing in trauma recovery, suicide prevention, and pastoral counseling. With a background in social work, mental health crisis intervention, and discipleship, he brings a unique perspective that integrates clinical wisdom with biblical truth. His is the owner and primary therapist for ThriveWell Counseling and Coaching Services.

Dr. Taylor is also an educator and author, serving as a Professor at Patten University, where he develops and teaches courses on Christian ministry leadership, marketplace ministry, counseling and cross-cultural evangelism. His academic background includes a Doctor of Ministry (DMin) with an emphasis in Clinical Mental Health and two Master of Arts degrees in Clinical and Mental Health Counseling as well as Discipleship and Ministry Leadership all from Pentecostal Theological Seminary (Cleveland, TN).

Through his own personal experiences of trauma, loss, and restoration, Dr. Taylor knows firsthand what it means to walk through the fire and come out refined. His journey has led him from the depths of despair—facing divorce, depression, and self-doubt—to a life fully redeemed by God's grace. His story is not just one of survival, but of thriving in the midst of brokenness and discovering that God truly brings beauty from the ashes.

He is deeply grateful for the unwavering support of his wife, Christy Taylor, who has stood beside him as both a partner in ministry and a living testament of God's grace. Together, they continue to serve, counsel, and equip individuals to overcome trauma, embrace healing, and walk in their God-given purpose.

Through Beauty from the Ashes: Breaking Through the Pain Where Grace Will Sustain, Dr. Taylor shares his heart, his struggles, and his testimony in hopes that others will find hope, healing, and the courage to step into their own redemptive story.

Connect with Dr. Mark A. Taylor:

thrivechurch

Thrive Church (Church of God)
www.thrivechurchvisalia.com
Visalia, CA

thrivewell
Counseling & Coaching Services

ThriveWell Counseling & Coaching Services
www.thrivewell.cc
Visalia, CA

Email/Phone
markt.beautyfromtheashes@gmail.com
559 510 0747